Artificial Intelligence with Python

A Practical Guide for Modern Development

By Scott Martin

Table of contents

Chapter 1: Python and Modern AI Setup

Chapter 2: Data Preparation for Machine Learning

Chapter 3: Supervised Learning: Regression and Classification

Chapter 4: Unsupervised Learning: Clustering and Dimensionality Reduction

- 4.1: Clustering Techniques: K-Means, Hierarchical Clustering
- 4.2: Dimensionality Reduction with PCA and Related Methods
- 4.3: Applications in Data Visualization and Anomaly Detection

Chapter 5: Deep Learning with TensorFlow and Keras

- 5.1: Building Neural Networks with Keras
- 5.2: Convolutional Neural Networks (CNNs) for Image Analysis
- 5.3: Recurrent Neural Networks (RNNs) for Sequence Data
- 5.4: Practical Image and Time-Series Projects

Chapter 6: Deep Learning with PyTorch

- 6.1: PyTorch Fundamentals and Tensor Operations
- 6.2: Building Custom Neural Network Architectures in PyTorch
- 6.3: CNNs and RNNs with PyTorch
- 6.4: TensorFlow vs. PyTorch: A Practical Comparison

Chapter 7: Generative AI and Large Language Models (LLMs)

- 7.1: Introduction to Transformers and LLM Architecture
- 7.2: Working with Pre-trained LLMs via Python APIs
- 7.3: Fine-tuning LLMs for Specific Tasks
- 7.4: Generative Adversarial Networks (GANs) and Variational Autoencoders (VAEs)

Chapter 8: Natural Language Processing (NLP) Applications

- 8.1: Text Preprocessing and Analysis with NLTK and spaCy
- 8.2: Sentiment Analysis, Text Classification, Summarization
- 8.3: Building Practical Chatbots and NLP Applications

Chapter 9: Reinforcement Learning in Practice

- 9.1: Q-Learning and Deep Reinforcement Learning
- 9.2: Practical Applications in Game Playing and Robotics

Chapter 10: AI Deployment and Scalability

- 10.1: Deploying AI Models to Cloud Platforms
- 10.2: Building Scalable AI Applications
- 10.3: Containerization with Docker for AI Deployment

Chapter 11: Ethical AI and Responsible Development

- 11.1: Addressing Bias and Fairness in AI Models
- 11.2: Ensuring Data Privacy and Security
- 11.3: Developing AI Responsibly and Ethically

Chapter 12: AI-Assisted Development Tools

- 12.1: Leveraging AI for Code Completion and Debugging
- 12.2: Integrating AI Tools into the Development Workflow
- 12.3: Staying Updated with Emerging AI Technologies

Chapter 13: Practical AI Projects and Exercises

-

Chapter 1: Python and Modern AI Setup

You're about to embark on a journey that's as exciting as it is powerful. Think of this chapter as your AI toolkit assembly. We'll get everything set up, explore why Python is your best friend in this adventure, and peek at the cool stuff happening in the AI world today. Let's make this fun and practical, okay?

1.1: What is Modern AI? Key Trends and Applications

Let's cut through the buzzwords and get down to what "modern AI" really means. It's not just a futuristic concept; it's a set of technologies reshaping our world right now.

Defining Modern AI: Beyond the Hype

At its core, modern AI is about creating systems that can perform tasks that typically require human intelligence. This includes learning, reasoning, problem-solving,and perception. But it's not just about mimicking humans; it's about pushing the boundaries of what's possible.

What sets modern AI apart? It's the convergence of several factors:

- **Vast Datasets:** We're generating more data than ever before, providing the fuel for AI models.
- **Computational Power:** Advances in hardware, especially GPUs, have made complex AI models feasible.
- **Sophisticated Algorithms:** Developments in deep learning and other techniques have unlocked new capabilities.

Key Trends Shaping Modern AI

Now, let's look at the trends driving this revolution:

- **Large Language Models (LLMs): The Power of Words:**
  - These models, like GPT-4 and Bard, are transforming how we interact with machines. They understand context, generate human-like text, and can even write code.
  - **Expert Commentary:** "LLMs are a paradigm shift. They're not just about generating text; they're about understanding and manipulating information in a way that was previously only possible for humans."

- **Generative AI: Creating from Scratch:**
  - This branch of AI focuses on generating new content, from images and music to code and design.GANs and VAEs are key players here.
  - **Personal Insight:** Witnessing the progression of generative models has been astounding. The ability of a machine to create novel content that is both realistic and artistic is something that I find incredibly fascinating.

- **AI-Assisted Development: The Programmer's Co-Pilot:**
  - Tools like GitHub Copilot are changing how we write code.They use AI to suggest completions, find bugs, and even generate entire functions.
  - **Concise Explanation:** This allows for much faster and more efficient coding, and can also help with learning new coding practices.

- **Reinforcement Learning: Learning Through Interaction:**
  - This technique trains agents to make decisions in an environment by rewarding desired behaviors. It's used in robotics, game playing, and autonomous systems.

- **Clear Language:** This is like teaching a computer by giving it rewards when it does something right.

Applications Across Industries

Modern AI is transforming every sector:

- **Healthcare:** AI is used for disease diagnosis, drug discovery, and personalized medicine.
- **Finance:** Algorithms are used for fraud detection, risk assessment, and algorithmic trading.
- **Transportation:** Self-driving cars and intelligent traffic management systems are becoming a reality.
- **Manufacturing:** AI is used for predictive maintenance and quality control.
- **Entertainment:** AI is used to create personalized recommendations and generate content.

The Ethical Considerations

It's important to acknowledge the ethical challenges that come with this powerful technology.

- **Bias and Fairness:** AI models can perpetuate and amplify existing biases.
- **Privacy and Security:** Protecting sensitive data is crucial.
- **Job Displacement:** Automation may lead to job losses in certain sectors.

Modern AI is not just a trend; it's a fundamental shift in how we interact with technology. By understanding its capabilities and limitations, we can harness its power to create a better future.

1.2: Why Python for AI Development Today?

If you're stepping into the world of artificial intelligence, you'll quickly realize that Python is the language everyone's talking about. But why? Let's break it down.

Python's Reign in the AI Realm: A Winning Combination

Python's popularity in AI isn't just a trend; it's a result of its unique blend of simplicity, a robust ecosystem, and a supportive community.

- **Simplicity and Readability: Writing Code That's Easy to Understand**
  - Python's clean and straightforward syntax makes it incredibly easy to learn and use, especially when dealing with complex AI algorithms.
  - **Expert Commentary:** "Python's readability is a major advantage. It allows developers, especially beginners, to focus on the core logic of their AI models instead of getting bogged down by intricate syntax."
- **A Vast Ecosystem of Libraries: Tools for Every AI Task**
  - Python has a massive collection of libraries specifically designed for AI and machine learning, making development faster and more efficient.
  - **Practical Implementation: Essential AI Libraries in Action**
- Python

Installing essential libraries (if not already installed)

pip install numpy pandas scikit-learn tensorflow torch transformers

Example 1: NumPy for Numerical Operations

```python
import numpy as np

# Creating a NumPy array

data = np.array([10, 20, 30, 40, 50])

# Calculating the mean

average = np.mean(data)

print(f"Average: {average}")

# Example 2: Pandas for Data Manipulation

import pandas as pd

# Creating a Pandas DataFrame

data = {'Name': ['Alice', 'Bob', 'Charlie'], 'Age': [25, 30, 28]}

df = pd.DataFrame(data)

print(df)

# Example 3: Scikit-learn for Basic Machine Learning
```

```python
from sklearn.linear_model import LinearRegression

# Sample data

x = np.array([[1], [2], [3], [4], [5]])  # Features

y = np.array([2, 4, 5, 4, 5])  # Target

# Creating and training the model

model = LinearRegression()

model.fit(x, y)

# Making a prediction

prediction = model.predict([[6]])

print(f"Prediction: {prediction}")

# Example 4: Transformers for Pre-trained Models

from transformers import pipeline

# Using a text generation pipeline
```

```python
generator = pipeline('text-generation', model='gpt2')

generated_text = generator("Python is great because", max_length=30,
num_return_sequences=1)[0]['generated_text']

print(generated_text)
```

```python
# Example 5: Tensorflow use.

import tensorflow as tf.
```

```python
print(f"Tensorflow Version: {tf.__version__}")
```

- **A Thriving and Supportive Community: Help Is Always at Hand**
  - Python boasts a large and active community, meaning you'll find ample resources, tutorials, and support online.
  - **Concise Explanation:** "This extensive community ensures that you're never alone on your AI journey. If you encounter a problem, chances are someone has already found a solution."
- **Versatility: Python's Applications Beyond AI**
  - Python's versatility extends beyond AI.It's a general-purpose language used for web development, data analysis, automation, and more.
  - **Personal Insight:** "The ability to use one language for everything from data preparation to model deployment streamlines the AI development process significantly. It reduces the need to switch between different languages and tools."

Why Now? The Perfect Conditions for Python AI

Python's dominance in AI is particularly pronounced today due to several factors:

- **The Deep Learning Revolution:** The rise of deep learning, with its complex neural networks, has favored Python's flexibility and ease of use.
- **The Open-Source Movement:** Python's open-source nature has fostered a culture of collaboration and rapid innovation in the AI community.
- **Cloud Computing and Scalability:** Cloud platforms have made it easier to deploy and scale Python-based AI applications, making them accessible to a wider audience.

Python, the Indispensable AI Tool

Python's simplicity, extensive libraries, and vibrant community have solidified its position as the go-to language for AI development.Whether you're a beginner or an experienced developer, Python provides the tools and resources you need to build powerful and impactful AI applications.

1.3: Setting Up Your Python AI Environment (Anaconda, VS Code, Cloud Options)

Before we dive into building AI models, we need to get our workspace ready. This section will guide you through setting up your Python AI environment using three popular options: Anaconda, VS Code, and cloud-based platforms.

Option 1: Anaconda - The All-in-One Solution

Anaconda is a Python distribution that comes pre-packaged with all the essential libraries for AI and data science. It simplifies the setup process and helps you manage your dependencies.

- **Step-by-Step Installation:**
    5. **Download:** Go to the Anaconda website (anaconda.com) and download the installer for your operating system.
    6. **Install:** Run the installer and follow the on-screen instructions.[1] Choose the default options for most settings.
    7. **Verify:** Open your terminal or command prompt and type conda --version. If Anaconda is installed correctly, you'll see the version number.
    8. **Create Environment:** Create a dedicated environment for your AI projects to avoid conflicts.
- Bash
    - conda create -n ai_env python=3.10 # Or the latest python version.
    - conda activate ai_env
    5. **Install Packages:** Install the necessary AI libraries.
- Bash
    - conda install numpy pandas scikit-learn tensorflow pytorch transformers
- **Expert Commentary:** "Anaconda is a fantastic starting point for beginners. It takes care of the complex dependency management, allowing you to focus on learning AI."

Option 2: VS Code - The Customizable Editor

Visual Studio Code (VS Code) is a powerful and versatile code editor that integrates seamlessly with Python. It's highly customizable and offers a wide range of extensions for AI development.

- **Step-by-Step Setup:**
    7. **Download and Install:** Download and install VS Code from code.visualstudio.com.
    8. **Install Python Extension:** Open VS Code, go to the Extensions tab (Ctrl+Shift+X), and search for "Python." Install the official Microsoft Python extension.
    9. **Install Python:** If you don't have Python installed, VS Code will prompt you to install it. Alternatively, install python from python.org.
    10. **Create Virtual Environment:** Create a virtual environment to isolate your project dependencies.
- Bash
    - python -m venv ai_venv

-
    7. **Activate Virtual Environment:** Activate the virtual environment.
    8. **Windows:** ai_venv\Scripts\activate
    9. **macOS/Linux:** source ai_venv/bin/activate
    10. **Install Packages:** Install the necessary AI libraries.
- Bash
    - pip install numpy pandas scikit-learn tensorflow torch transformers
    7. **Select Interpreter:** In VS Code, select the Python interpreter from your virtual environment.

- **Personal Insight:** "VS Code's flexibility and extensive extension ecosystem make it my go-to editor for AI development. The ability to customize it to my specific needs is a huge advantage."

Option 3: Cloud Options (Google Colab) - The Browser-Based Solution

Google Colab is a free, cloud-based platform that provides access to GPUs and TPUs. It's an excellent option for beginners who don't want to install anything on their local machines.

- **Step-by-Step Usage:**
    4. **Go to Colab:** Open your web browser and go to colab.research.google.com.
    5. **Create a New Notebook:** Create a new Python 3 notebook.
    6. **Install Packages:** Install the necessary AI libraries using pip within the notebook.
- Python
    - !pip install numpy pandas scikit-learn tensorflow torch transformers
-
    4. **Use GPUs/TPUs:** Change the runtime type to GPU or TPU in the "Runtime" menu.
    5. **Code:** Start writing your Python AI code directly in the notebook cells.
- **Concise Explanation:** "Colab is perfect for quick prototyping and learning. It eliminates the hassle of local setup and provides access to powerful hardware for free."

Practical Implementation: Testing Your Setup

Regardless of which option you choose, let's test your setup with a simple code snippet.

Python

```
import tensorflow as tf
import torch
from transformers import pipeline

print(f"TensorFlow version: {tf.__version__}")
print(f"PyTorch version: {torch.__version__}")

generator = pipeline('text-generation', model='gpt2')
print(generator("Hello, AI world!", max_length=30,
    num_return_sequences=1)[0]['generated_text'])
```

If you see the TensorFlow and PyTorch versions and the generated text, your setup is successful!

Your AI Workspace is Ready

You've now successfully set up your Python AI environment. Whether you chose Anaconda, VS Code, or Google Colab, you're ready to start building amazing AI applications.

1.4: Essential Python Libraries: NumPy, Pandas, Matplotlib, Seaborn

Before we build sophisticated AI models, we need to master the fundamental tools for data manipulation and visualization. In this section, we'll explore four essential Python libraries: NumPy, Pandas, Matplotlib, and Seaborn.

NumPy: The Numerical Powerhouse

NumPy is the cornerstone of numerical computing in Python. It provides powerful tools for working with arrays and matrices.

- **Arrays and Matrices:**
    - NumPy's ndarray (n-dimensional array) is the core data structure. It's much faster and more efficient than Python lists for numerical operations.
    - **Practical Implementation:**
- Python
- import numpy as np
-
- # Creating a NumPy array
- arr = np.array([1, 2, 3, 4, 5])
- print("NumPy Array:", arr)
-
- # Performing mathematical operations
- mean = np.mean(arr)
- std_dev = np.std(arr)
- print("Mean:", mean)
- print("Standard Deviation:", std_dev)
-

- # Creating a 2D array (matrix)
- matrix = np.array([[1, 2, 3], [4, 5, 6]])
- print("Matrix:\n", matrix)
-
- # Matrix multiplication
- matrix_transpose = matrix.T
- matrix_product = np.dot(matrix, matrix_transpose)
- print("Matrix Product:\n", matrix_product)
- **Expert Commentary:** "NumPy's efficiency is crucial for AI, where we often deal with large datasets and complex numerical computations. It's the engine that powers many other AI libraries."

Pandas: Data Manipulation Made Easy

Pandas is a powerful library for data analysis and manipulation. It provides data structures like DataFrames and Series, which make working with tabular data a breeze.

- **DataFrames and Series:**
  - DataFrames are 2D tables, and Series are 1D labeled arrays.
  - **Practical Implementation:**
- Python
- import pandas as pd
-
- # Creating a Pandas DataFrame
- data = {'Name': ['Alice', 'Bob', 'Charlie'],
-     'Age': [25, 30, 28],
-     'City': ['New York', 'London', 'Tokyo']}

- df = pd.DataFrame(data)
- print("DataFrame:\n", df)
-
- # Selecting data
- ages = df['Age']
- print("Ages:\n", ages)
-
- # Filtering data
- london_people = df[df['City'] == 'London']
- print("London People:\n", london_people)
-
- # Grouping and aggregating data
- age_groups = df.groupby('City')['Age'].mean()
- print("Average Ages by City:\n", age_groups)
-
-
- **Personal Insight:** "Pandas transformed how I work with data. Its intuitive syntax and powerful features make data cleaning and analysis much more efficient and enjoyable."

Matplotlib: Basic Data Visualization

Matplotlib is a fundamental library for creating static, interactive, and animated visualizations in Python.

- **Plots and Charts:**
  - Matplotlib allows you to create various types of plots, including line plots, scatter plots, bar charts, and histograms.

     ○ **Practical Implementation:**

- Python
- import matplotlib.pyplot as plt
-
- # Creating a line plot
- x = np.linspace(0, 10, 100)
- y = np.sin(x)
- plt.plot(x, y)
- plt.title('Sine Wave')
- plt.xlabel('X-axis')
- plt.ylabel('Y-axis')
- plt.show()
-
- # Creating a scatter plot
- plt.scatter(df['Age'], range(len(df)))
- plt.title("Scatter Plot of Age")
- plt.show()
-
-
- **Concise Explanation:** "Matplotlib is essential for visualizing data and gaining insights. It's the foundation for many other visualization libraries."

Seaborn: Enhanced Data Visualization

Seaborn is a higher-level visualization library built on top of Matplotlib. It provides a more aesthetically pleasing and statistically informative way to visualize data.

- **Statistical Plots:**

- ○ Seaborn simplifies the creation of complex statistical plots, such as violin plots, box plots, and heatmaps.
  - ○ **Practical Implementation:**
- Python
- import seaborn as sns
-
- # Creating a violin plot
- sns.violinplot(x='City', y='Age', data=df)
- plt.title('Age Distribution by City')
- plt.show()
-
- # Creating a heatmap
- correlation_matrix = df[['Age']].corr()
- sns.heatmap(correlation_matrix, annot=True)
- plt.titlc('Correlation Heatmap')
- plt.show()
- **Expert Commentary:** "Seaborn's ability to create beautiful and informative statistical plots makes it an invaluable tool for data analysis and presentation."

Your Data Toolkit is Complete!

You've now mastered the essential Python libraries for data manipulation and visualization. NumPy, Pandas, Matplotlib, and Seaborn will be your trusty companions as you explore the world of AI. Let's move on to the next section and learn how to utilize Jupyter Notebooks and Google Colab for interactive development.

1.5: Utilizing Jupyter Notebooks and Google Colab

Hey there, interactive coders! In this section, we'll explore two powerful tools that make coding and experimenting with AI incredibly efficient: Jupyter Notebooks and Google Colab. These environments allow you to write code, visualize data, and document your work all in one place.

Jupyter Notebooks: Your Interactive Coding Playground

Jupyter Notebooks are web-based interactive computational environments that allow you to create and share documents that contain live code, equations, visualizations, and narrative text.

- **Step-by-Step Usage:**
    1. **Installation (if needed):** If you're using Anaconda, Jupyter Notebooks are already installed. If not, install it using pip install notebook.
    2. **Launching Jupyter:** Open your terminal or command prompt and type jupyter notebook. This will open a new tab in your web browser.
    3. **Creating a New Notebook:** Click "New" and select "Python 3" (or your Python environment).
    4. **Writing Code:** Write your Python code in code cells and press Shift+Enter to execute them.
    5. **Adding Markdown:** Add markdown cells for documentation and explanations.
    6. **Visualizing Data:** Use Matplotlib or Seaborn to visualize your data directly in the notebook.
    7. **Saving and Sharing:** Save your notebook as a .ipynb file and share it with others.

- **Practical Implementation:**
- Python
- # Code Cell 1: Import Libraries
- import numpy as np
- import pandas as pd
- import matplotlib.pyplot as plt
- import seaborn as sns
-
- # Code Cell 2: Create a DataFrame
- data = {'Name': ['Alice', 'Bob', 'Charlie'],
-     'Age': [25, 30, 28],
-     'City': ['New York', 'London', 'Tokyo']}
- df = pd.DataFrame(data)
-
- # Code Cell 3: Display the DataFrame
- print(df)
-
- # Code Cell 4: Create a Scatter Plot
- plt.scatter(df['Age'], range(len(df)))
- plt.title("Scatter Plot of Age")
- plt.show()
-
- # Markdown Cell: Add an explanation
- # This scatter plot shows the distribution of ages in our DataFrame.
-
-

- **Expert Commentary:** "Jupyter Notebooks are essential for interactive data analysis and exploration. They allow you to quickly iterate on your code and visualize your results, making the development process more efficient."

Google Colab: Your Cloud-Powered Notebook

Google Colab is a free, cloud-based Jupyter Notebook environment that provides access to GPUs and TPUs. It's perfect for running computationally intensive AI tasks.

- **Step-by-Step Usage:**
  1. **Go to Colab:** Open your web browser and go to colab.research.google.com.
  2. **Create a New Notebook:** Create a new Python 3 notebook.
  3. **Writing Code:** Write your Python code in code cells and press Shift+Enter to execute them.
  4. **Adding Markdown:** Add markdown cells for documentation and explanations.
  5. **Using GPUs/TPUs:** Change the runtime type to GPU or TPU in the "Runtime" menu.
  6. **Installing Packages:** Install any necessary packages using !pip install in a code cell.
  7. **Saving and Sharing:** Your notebooks are automatically saved to Google Drive, and you can share them with others.
- **Practical Implementation (Google Colab):**
- Python
- # Code Cell 1: Install Libraries
- !pip install numpy pandas matplotlib seaborn

-
- # Code Cell 2: Import Libraries
- import numpy as np
- import pandas as pd
- import matplotlib.pyplot as plt
- import seaborn as sns
-
- # Code Cell 3: Create a DataFrame
- data = {'Name': ['Alice', 'Bob', 'Charlie'],
-     'Age': [25, 30, 28],
-     'City': ['New York', 'London', 'Tokyo']}
- df = pd.DataFrame(data)
-
- # Code Cell 4: Display the DataFrame
- print(df)
-
- # Code Cell 5: Create a Seaborn Violin Plot
- sns.violinplot(x='City', y='Age', data=df)
- plt.title('Age Distribution by City')
- plt.show()
-
- # Markdown Cell: Add an explanation
- # This violin plot shows the age distribution for each city in our DataFrame.
-
-
- **Personal Insight:** "Google Colab is a game-changer for AI development. The ability to access GPUs and TPUs for free makes it accessible to

everyone, regardless of their hardware setup. It's also great for collaborative projects."

Key Advantages:

- **Interactive Development:** Write and execute code in real-time.
- **Data Visualization:** Visualize data directly in the notebook.
- **Documentation:** Combine code, explanations, and visualizations in one document.
- **Collaboration:** Share notebooks easily with others.
- **Cloud Access (Colab):** Access powerful hardware without local setup.

Jupyter Notebooks and Google Colab provide an interactive and efficient environment for AI development. They allow you to write code, visualize data, and document your work all in one place, making the development process more enjoyable and productive. Let's move on to the next section and explore Python 3.13 performance considerations for AI.

1.6: Python 3.13 Performance Considerations for AI

With the release of Python 3.13, we're seeing some promising performance improvements, especially for AI workloads. Let's delve into how these changes can impact your AI projects and how to leverage them.

Python 3.13: A Boost for AI?

Python has often been criticized for its Global Interpreter Lock (GIL), which limits the execution of multiple threads in parallel. Python 3.13 introduces some experimental features that seek to address this, and other general performance improvements.

- **Experimental Free-Threaded Mode:**
  - Python 3.13 introduces an experimental free-threaded mode. This mode aims to remove the GIL, allowing for true parallelism.
  - **Expert Commentary:** "This is a significant development for Python. While still experimental, the potential for increased parallelism in AI workloads is substantial. This change has the potential to drastically reduce the time needed to train large models."
  - **Practical Implications:**
    - For AI tasks that involve heavy parallel computations, such as neural network training, this could lead to significant speedups.
    - Libraries like TensorFlow and PyTorch, which rely on parallel processing, could benefit greatly.
    - **Important Considerations:**
      - This is an experimental feature, and its behavior and performance may change in future releases.
      - Not all Python code will benefit equally from this mode. Code that is heavily I/O bound, for example, may not see much improvement.
- **General Performance Improvements:**
  - Python 3.13 also includes various other performance optimizations, such as improved memory management and faster execution of certain operations.

- ○ **Practical Implications:**
  - These general improvements can benefit a wide range of AI tasks, from data preprocessing to model inference.
  - Even without the free-threaded mode, you may see noticeable speedups in your AI code.
- **Leveraging Performance Improvements:**
  - ○ **Vectorization:** Vectorization with NumPy remains a key optimization technique.
  - ○ **Example:**
- Python

```
import numpy as np

import time


# Using NumPy for vectorized operations

def vectorized_sum(arr):

    return np.sum(arr)


# Using a loop for element-wise sum

def loop_sum(arr):

    total = 0
```

```python
    for x in arr:

        total += x

    return total


arr = np.random.rand(1000000)


start_time = time.time()

vectorized_result = vectorized_sum(arr)

vectorized_time = time.time() - start_time


start_time = time.time()

loop_result = loop_sum(arr)

loop_time = time.time() - start_time


print(f"Vectorized Time: {vectorized_time} seconds")

print(f"Loop Time: {loop_time} seconds")
```

- **GPU Acceleration:** Utilize GPU acceleration with libraries like TensorFlow and PyTorch.
- **Example (TensorFlow):**

```
import tensorflow as tf

# Check if GPU is available

print("Num GPUs Available: ", len(tf.config.list_physical_devices('GPU')))


# Example of using a GPU for computation

if tf.config.list_physical_devices('GPU'):

    with tf.device('/GPU:0'):

        a = tf.random.normal((1000, 1000))

        b = tf.random.normal((1000, 1000))

        c = tf.matmul(a, b)

        print("GPU computation successful.")
```
```

* **Profiling:** Use profiling tools to identify performance bottlenecks in your AI code.

**Personal Insight:** "The improvements in python 3.13 represent a very exciting time for python based AI. The ability to utilize more of the computers resources, will lead to faster model training, and faster data processing. It is very important to stay up to date with the latest python versions."

Python 3.13 brings performance enhancements that can benefit AI workloads. By leveraging the experimental free-threaded mode, utilizing GPU acceleration, and
```

optimizing your code, you can build faster and more efficient AI applications. Keep an eye on future Python releases for further performance improvements.

Chapter 2: Data Preparation for Machine Learning

Now that we've got our Python AI workshop set up, it's time to talk about the raw material we'll be working with: data. Think of data as the paint and canvas for your AI masterpieces. Without good data, your models won't be able to create anything meaningful. This chapter is all about getting your data ready for the exciting journey ahead.

2.1: Data Acquisition: APIs, Web Scraping, Databases

Before we can train our AI models, we need data. And lots of it. This section will guide you through the primary ways of acquiring data: APIs, web scraping, and databases.

Data Acquisition: The Foundation of AI

The quality and quantity of your data directly impact the performance of your AI models.Let's explore the methods to gather this crucial resource.

- **APIs (Application Programming Interfaces): Your Data Pipeline**
    - APIs provide a structured way to access data from various online services.Think of them as a contract: you ask for specific data, and the API delivers it in a predictable format (often JSON or XML).
    - **Expert Commentary:** "APIs are the gold standard for data acquisition. They offer reliable and up-to-date data, often with clear documentation.If available, always prioritize APIs."
    - **Practical Implementation: Using the Requests Library**
- Python

```python
import requests

import json


# Example: Fetching data from a public API (e.g., OpenWeatherMap)

api_key = "YOUR_API_KEY"  # Replace with your actual API key

city = "London"

url = f"http://api.openweathermap.org/data/2.5/weather?q={city}&appid={api_key}"


try:

    response = requests.get(url)

    response.raise_for_status()  # Raise an exception for bad status codes (4xx or 5xx)

    data = response.json()

    print(json.dumps(data, indent=4)) #prints the json in a pretty format.

    temperature = data["main"]["temp"]

    print(f"Temperature in {city}: {temperature} K")


except requests.exceptions.RequestException as e:
```

```python
    print(f"An error occurred: {e}")

except KeyError:

    print("Invalid API response format")
```

-
  - **Note:** You'll need an API key from OpenWeatherMap (or another service) to run this code.[5] Remember to handle potential errors.
- **Web Scraping: Extracting Data from Websites**
  - When APIs aren't available, web scraping allows you to extract data directly from website HTML. This involves parsing the HTML structure and extracting the desired information.
  - **Personal Insight:** "Web scraping can be a powerful tool, but it's essential to respect website terms of service and robots.txt. Always scrape responsibly and avoid overloading servers."
  - **Practical Implementation: Using Beautiful Soup and Requests**
- Python

```python
import requests

from bs4 import BeautifulSoup


# Example: Scraping titles from a website

url = "https://www.example.com"  # Replace with the website you want to scrape
```

```python
try:

    response = requests.get(url)

    response.raise_for_status()

    soup = BeautifulSoup(response.content, "html.parser")

    titles = soup.find_all("title")

    for title in titles:

        print(title.text)


except requests.exceptions.RequestException as e:

    print(f"An error occured: {e}")
```

- ○ **Note:** Be mindful of website structure changes, as they can break your scraper.
- **Databases: Structured Data Storage**
  - ○ Databases are used to store and manage structured data. You might need to connect to a database to retrieve data for your AI projects, especially in enterprise environments.
  - ○ **Concise Explanation:** "Databases offer organized and efficient data storage, crucial for large-scale AI applications. Python libraries like sqlite3 (for SQLite), psycopg2 (for PostgreSQL), and mysql-connector-python (for MySQL) facilitate database interaction."
  - ○ **Practical Implementation: Using SQLite3**
- Python

```python
import sqlite3

# Example: Connecting to an SQLite database and retrieving data

try:

    conn = sqlite3.connect("my_database.db")  # Creates or connects to the database

    cursor = conn.cursor()


    # Execute a query

    cursor.execute("SELECT * FROM my_table")

    rows = cursor.fetchall()


    for row in rows:

        print(row)


    conn.close()


except sqlite3.Error as e:

    print(f"An error occured: {e}")
```

○ **Note:** This example assumes you have an SQLite database named my_database.db with a table named my_table.

Key Considerations:

- **Data Quality:** Ensure the data you acquire is accurate, complete, and relevant to your AI project.
- **Legal and Ethical Considerations:** Respect data privacy, comply with regulations, and avoid scraping copyrighted or sensitive information.
- **Data Volume:** Choose the appropriate acquisition method based on the volume and frequency of data you need.

You've now learned the key methods for acquiring data for your AI projects. APIs, web scraping, and databases provide access to a wealth of information. Choose the methods that best suit your needs and always prioritize data quality and ethical considerations.

2.2: Modern Data Cleaning and Preprocessing with Pandas

We've got our data, but it's rarely in perfect shape. This section is all about using Pandas to clean and preprocess our data, making it ready for AI models.

Pandas: Your Data Cleaning Power Tool

Pandas is indispensable for data cleaning and preprocessing. It provides powerful tools to handle missing values, inconsistencies, and other data quality issues.

- **Loading Data:**
    - Pandas can read data from various file formats (CSV, Excel, JSON, etc.).
    - **Practical Implementation:**
- Python
- import pandas as pd
-
- # Example: Loading a CSV file
- try:
-     df = pd.read_csv("data.csv") # Replace with your file path
-     print("Data loaded successfully.")
-     print(df.head()) #shows the top 5 rows of the dataframe.
-
- except FileNotFoundError:
-     print("File not found. Please check the file path.")
- **Handling Missing Values:**
    - Missing values (NaNs) are common. Pandas offers methods to handle them.
    - **Practical Implementation:**
- Python
- # Example: Checking for missing values
- print("Missing values per column:\n", df.isnull().sum())
-
- # Example: Filling missing values with the mean
- df['Age'].fillna(df['Age'].mean(), inplace=True)
-
- # Example: Dropping rows with missing values

- df.dropna(inplace=True

- **Data Formatting and Transformation:**
  - Ensuring data is in the correct format is crucial.
  - **Practical Implementation:**

- Python

- # Example: Converting data types

- df['Date'] = pd.to_datetime(df['Date']) #if 'Date' column exists.

-

- # Example: Applying a function to a column

- def categorize_age(age):

-   if age < 18:

-     return "Minor"

-   elif age < 65:

-     return "Adult"

-   else:

-     return "Senior"

-

- df['Age_Category'] = df['Age'].apply(categorize_age)

-

- #Example: Scaling numerical data.

- from sklearn.preprocessing import StandardScaler

-

- scaler = StandardScaler()

- df[["age_scaled"]] = scaler.fit_transform(df[["Age"]])

- **Removing Duplicates and Outliers:**
  - Duplicates and outliers can skew your analysis.
  - **Practical Implementation:**

- Python
- # Example: Removing duplicate rows
- df.drop_duplicates(inplace=True)
-
- # Example: Removing outliers (using IQR method)
- Q1 = df['Value'].quantile(0.25)
- Q3 = df['Value'].quantile(0.75)
- IQR = Q3 - Q1
- df = df[~((df['Value'] < (Q1 - 1.5 * IQR)) | (df['Value'] > (Q3 + 1.5 * IQR)))]
-
-
-

- **Text Preprocessing:**
  - For text data, we need to clean and normalize it.
  - **Practical Implementation:**
- Python
- import re
-
- def clean_text(text):
-     text = text.lower()
-     text = re.sub(r'[^a-zA-Z0-9\s]', '', text)
-     return text
-
- df['Text_Clean'] = df['Text'].apply(clean_text)
- **Expert Commentary:** "Pandas' ability to handle diverse data cleaning tasks efficiently is invaluable. It transforms raw data into a usable format, saving significant time and effort in AI projects."

- **Personal Insight:** "When I first started, cleaning data felt like a chore, but Pandas made it much more manageable. The ability to chain multiple operations together makes complex cleaning tasks surprisingly straightforward."

Key Considerations:

- **Data Understanding:** Understand your data's characteristics and potential issues.
- **Data Integrity:** Ensure data cleaning doesn't introduce new errors.
- **Reproducibility:** Document your cleaning steps for reproducibility.

By mastering Pandas for data cleaning and preprocessing, you'll be able to prepare your data for effective AI model training. Remember to always understand your data and document your steps. Let's move onto feature engineering.

2.3: Feature Engineering for Enhanced Model Performance

We've cleaned our data, and now it's time to get creative. Feature engineering is the art of transforming raw data into features that better represent the underlying problem to the predictive models, resulting in improved model accuracy on unseen data.

Feature Engineering: The Art of Data Transformation

Feature engineering is a crucial step in the machine learning pipeline. It's about creating new features or modifying existing ones to make your models more effective.

- **Creating New Features:**
  - Combine existing features to create new ones that capture more information.
  - **Practical Implementation:**
- Python
- import pandas as pd
-
- # Example: Creating a new feature by combining existing ones
- data = {'bedrooms': [2, 3, 4, 2, 5],
-     'bathrooms': [1, 2, 2, 1, 3],
-     'square_feet': [1000, 1500, 2000, 1200, 2500],
-     'price': [200000, 300000, 400000, 250000, 500000]}
- df = pd.DataFrame(data)
-
- # Create a new feature: price per square foot
- df['price_per_sqft'] = df['price'] / df['square_feet']
- print(df.head())
-
-
- **Encoding Categorical Variables:**
  - Machine learning models typically work with numerical data.[7] We need to encode categorical variables.
  - **Practical Implementation:**
- Python
- # Example: One-hot encoding
- df = pd.get_dummies(df, columns=['bedrooms'], prefix='bedrooms')
- print(df.head())

-
- # Example: Label encoding
- from sklearn.preprocessing import LabelEncoder
-
- le = LabelEncoder()
- df['city_encoded'] = le.fit_transform(df['city']) # if 'city' column exists.
- print(df.head())
- **Scaling Numerical Features:**
  - Scaling numerical features to a similar range can improve model performance.
  - **Practical Implementation:**
- Python
- # Example: Standard scaling
- from sklearn.preprocessing import StandardScaler
-
- scaler = StandardScaler()
- df[['square_feet_scaled']] = scaler.fit_transform(df[['square_feet']])
- print(df.head())
-
- #Example: MinMax Scaling.
- from sklearn.preprocessing import MinMaxScaler
-
- min_max_scaler = MinMaxScaler()
- df[['price_scaled']] = min_max_scaler.fit_transform(df[['price']])
- print(df.head())
-
-

- **Handling Date and Time Features:**
  - Extract meaningful information from date and time features.
  - **Practical Implementation:**
- Python
- # Example: Extracting day of the week
- df['date'] = pd.to_datetime(df['date']) # if 'date' column exists.
- df['day_of_week'] = df['date'].dt.day_name()
- print(df.head())
-
-

- **Polynomial Features:**
  - Create polynomial features to capture non-linear relationships.
  - **Practical Implementation:**
- Python
- # Example: Creating polynomial features
- from sklearn.preprocessing import PolynomialFeatures
-
- poly = PolynomialFeatures(degree=2)
- poly_features = poly.fit_transform(df[['square_feet']])
- print(poly_features)
-
-

- **Expert Commentary:** "Feature engineering is where domain knowledge meets data science.It's about understanding the underlying problem and creating features that capture the essential information."
- **Personal Insight:** "When I first started, I underestimated the power of feature engineering. But I quickly realized that it can make a bigger

difference than trying different models. It's about telling the story of your data in a way that the model understands."

Key Considerations:

- **Domain Knowledge:** Use your understanding of the problem domain to guide feature engineering.
- **Feature Importance:** Use techniques like feature importance from tree-based models to identify important features.
- **Overfitting:** Avoid creating too many features, as it can lead to overfitting.
- **Experimentation:** Feature engineering is an iterative process. Experiment with different techniques and evaluate their impact on model performance.

2.4: Efficient Handling of Large Datasets

We've tackled data cleaning and feature engineering, but what happens when our datasets become massive? This section will guide you through techniques for efficiently handling large datasets, ensuring your AI projects remain performant and manageable.

Handling Large Datasets: Scaling Your Data Processing

Large datasets present unique challenges, including memory limitations and processing bottlenecks. Let's explore strategies to overcome these hurdles.

- **Chunking and Iteration:**
  - Instead of loading the entire dataset into memory, we can process it in smaller chunks.
  - **Practical Implementation:**
- Python

```python
import pandas as pd

# Example: Reading a large CSV file in chunks

chunk_size = 10000  # Number of rows per chunk

reader = pd.read_csv("large_data.csv", chunksize=chunk_size)


for chunk in reader:
    # Process each chunk
    print(f"Processing chunk with {len(chunk)} rows.")
    # Perform operations on the chunk (e.g., data cleaning, aggregation)
    # ...
```

- o **Expert Commentary:** "Chunking is essential for datasets that exceed available memory. It allows you to process data incrementally, reducing memory footprint."
- **Optimized Data Types:**
  - o Using the appropriate data types can significantly reduce memory usage.
  - o **Practical Implementation:**
- Python

```python
import pandas as pd
```

```python
import numpy as np

# Example: Converting data types to reduce memory usage

df = pd.read_csv("large_data.csv")


# Check memory usage

print(f"Original memory usage: {df.memory_usage(deep=True).sum() / (1024 * 1024):.2f} MB")


# Convert numeric columns to smaller data types

numeric_cols = df.select_dtypes(include=np.number).columns

for col in numeric_cols:

    if df[col].max() < 255 and df[col].min() >= 0:

        df[col] = pd.to_numeric(df[col], downcast='unsigned')

    else:

        df[col] = pd.to_numeric(df[col], downcast='integer')


# Convert categorical columns to category type
```

```python
categorical_cols = df.select_dtypes(include='object').columns

for col in categorical_cols:

    df[col] = df[col].astype('category')


# Check memory usage after optimization

print(f"Optimized memory usage: {df.memory_usage(deep=True).sum() / (1024 * 1024):.2f} MB")
```

- **Data Sampling:**
  - If the dataset is too large, consider working with a representative sample.
  - **Practical Implementation:**
- Python

```python
import pandas as pd


# Example: Sampling a portion of the dataset

df = pd.read_csv("large_data.csv")

sample_size = 0.1  # 10% sample

sampled_df = df.sample(frac=sample_size, random_state=42)

print(f"Sampled DataFrame shape: {sampled_df.shape}")
```

- **Using Dask or Spark:**
  - For extremely large datasets, consider using distributed computing frameworks like Dask or Spark.
  - **Concise Explanation:** "Dask and Spark allow you to process data in parallel across multiple machines, significantly speeding up processing time. They are invaluable for datasets that don't fit into a single machine's memory."
  - **Practical Implementation (Dask):**
- Python

```
import dask.dataframe as dd


# Example: Reading a large CSV file with Dask

ddf = dd.read_csv("large_data.csv")


# Perform operations on the Dask DataFrame

mean_value = ddf['column_name'].mean().compute() #compute is important.

print(f"Mean value: {mean_value}")
```

- **Out-of-Core Processing:**
  - Libraries like vaex allow you to work with datasets larger than your RAM by using memory mapping and lazy evaluation.

○ **Personal Insight:** "I was initially intimidated by the sheer size of some datasets, but tools like Dask and Vaex made it possible to tackle them efficiently. They allowed me to focus on the analysis rather than the technical limitations."

Key Considerations:

- **Data Format:** Consider using efficient data formats like Parquet or Feather.
- **Hardware:** Leverage powerful hardware with sufficient RAM and processing power.
- **Parallel Processing:** Utilize parallel processing techniques to speed up computations.
- **Profiling:** Profile your code to identify performance bottlenecks.

Chapter 3: Supervised Learning: Regression and Classification

Now that we've got our data prepped and ready, it's time to dive into the heart of machine learning: supervised learning. This is where we teach machines to make predictions based on labeled data. In this chapter, we'll explore two fundamental types of supervised learning: regression (predicting continuous values) and classification (predicting categories). Let's make some predictions!

3.1: Practical Implementation of Regression Algorithms

We're stepping into the realm of supervised learning, and regression is our first stop. This section will guide you through the practical implementation of regression algorithms, using Python and scikit-learn.

Regression: Predicting Continuous Values

Regression algorithms are used to predict continuous numerical values, like house prices, stock values, or temperature. Let's get our hands dirty with some code.

- **Linear Regression: The Foundation**
  - Linear regression models the relationship between the independent variable(s) and the dependent variable using a linear equation.
  - **Practical Implementation:**
- Python

```
import numpy as np

import pandas as pd
```

```python
from sklearn.model_selection import train_test_split

from sklearn.linear_model import LinearRegression

from sklearn.metrics import mean_squared_error, r2_score


# Sample data

data = {'X': [1, 2, 3, 4, 5], 'Y': [2, 4, 5, 4, 5]}

df = pd.DataFrame(data)


# Prepare data

X = df[['X']]  # Features

y = df['Y']     # Target


# Split data into training and testing sets

X_train, X_test, y_train, y_test = train_test_split(X, y, test_size=0.2,
random_state=42)


# Create and train the model

model = LinearRegression()
```

```python
model.fit(X_train, y_train)


# Make predictions

y_pred = model.predict(X_test)


# Evaluate the model

mse = mean_squared_error(y_test, y_pred)

r2 = r2_score(y_test, y_pred)


print(f"Mean Squared Error: {mse}")

print(f"R-squared: {r2}")
```

-
  - **Expert Commentary:** "Linear regression is simple yet powerful. It's a great starting point for regression tasks and provides a baseline for comparison with more complex models."
- **Polynomial Regression: Capturing Non-Linear Relationships**
  - Polynomial regression extends linear regression by allowing for polynomial relationships between variables.
  - **Practical Implementation:**
- Python

```python
from sklearn.preprocessing import PolynomialFeatures

# Create polynomial features

poly = PolynomialFeatures(degree=2)

X_poly = poly.fit_transform(X)


# Split data

X_train_poly, X_test_poly, y_train, y_test = train_test_split(X_poly, y,
test_size=0.2, random_state=42)


# Train the model

poly_model = LinearRegression()

poly_model.fit(X_train_poly, y_train)


# Make predictions

y_poly_pred = poly_model.predict(X_test_poly)


# Evaluate the model
```

```
poly_mse = mean_squared_error(y_test, y_poly_pred)
```

```
poly_r2 = r2_score(y_test, y_poly_pred)
```

```
print(f"Polynomial Mean Squared Error: {poly_mse}")
```

```
print(f"Polynomial R-squared: {poly_r2}")
```

- **Ridge and Lasso Regression: Regularization Techniques**
  - Ridge and Lasso regression are linear regression variants that add regularization terms to prevent overfitting.
  - **Practical Implementation:**
- Python

```
from sklearn.linear_model import Ridge, Lasso
```

```
# Ridge Regression
```

```
ridge_model = Ridge(alpha=1.0) #alpha controls the regularization strength.
```

```
ridge_model.fit(X_train, y_train)
```

```
ridge_pred = ridge_model.predict(X_test)
```

```
ridge_mse = mean_squared_error(y_test, ridge_pred)
```

```
print(f"Ridge Mean Squared Error: {ridge_mse}")
```

```
# Lasso Regression

lasso_model = Lasso(alpha=1.0)

lasso_model.fit(X_train, y_train)

lasso_pred = lasso_model.predict(X_test)

lasso_mse = mean_squared_error(y_test, lasso_pred)

print(f"Lasso Mean Squared Error: {lasso_mse}")
```

- **Personal Insight:** "I remember when I first started, I was amazed at how simple linear regression could be. But then I discovered polynomial regression and regularization, which allowed me to model more complex relationships and prevent overfitting. It was like unlocking a new level of predictive power."

Key Considerations:

- **Data Preprocessing:** Ensure your data is clean and preprocessed before training the model.
- **Feature Selection:** Select relevant features to improve model performance.
- **Model Evaluation:** Use appropriate metrics (MSE, R-squared) to evaluate model performance.
- **Hyperparameter Tuning:** Tune hyperparameters (e.g., alpha in Ridge and Lasso) to optimize model performance.

You've now learned how to implement various regression algorithms using scikit-learn. Remember to preprocess your data, select relevant features, and evaluate your model's performance. Let's move on to classification algorithms.

3.2: Classification Algorithms: Logistic Regression, SVM, Trees, Boosting

We're now diving into the world of classification, where our goal is to predict categorical labels. This section will guide you through the practical implementation of various classification algorithms, using Python and scikit-learn.

Classification: Predicting Categories

Classification algorithms are used to predict discrete categories, such as spam/not spam, cat/dog, or fraud/not fraud.Let's explore some key algorithms.

- **Logistic Regression: The Binary Classifier**
  - Despite its name, logistic regression is a classification algorithm used for binary classification problems.
  - **Practical Implementation:**
- Python

```
import pandas as pd

from sklearn.model_selection import train_test_split

from sklearn.linear_model import LogisticRegression

from sklearn.metrics import accuracy_score, classification_report


# Sample data (binary classification)

data = {'X1': [1, 2, 3, 4, 5], 'X2': [2, 3, 4, 5, 6], 'Y': [0, 0, 1, 1, 1]}
```

```python
df = pd.DataFrame(data)


# Prepare data

X = df[['X1', 'X2']]  # Features

y = df['Y']          # Target


# Split data

X_train, X_test, y_train, y_test = train_test_split(X, y, test_size=0.2,
random_state=42)


# Create and train the model

model = LogisticRegression()

model.fit(X_train, y_train)


# Make predictions

y_pred = model.predict(X_test)


# Evaluate the model
```

```
accuracy = accuracy_score(y_test, y_pred)

report = classification_report(y_test, y_pred)
```

```
print(f"Accuracy: {accuracy}")

print(f"Classification Report:\n{report}")
```

- Expert Commentary: "Logistic regression is a fundamental algorithm for binary classification. It's simple, efficient, and provides interpretable results."
- **Support Vector Machines (SVM): Finding the Optimal Boundary**
  - SVMs find the optimal hyperplane that best separates the classes in the feature space.
  - **Practical Implementation:**
    - Python

```
from sklearn.svm import SVC
```

```
# Create and train the model

svm_model = SVC()

svm_model.fit(X_train, y_train)
```

```
# Make predictions
```

```python
svm_pred = svm_model.predict(X_test)


# Evaluate the model

svm_accuracy = accuracy_score(y_test, svm_pred)

svm_report = classification_report(y_test, svm_pred)


print(f"SVM Accuracy: {svm_accuracy}")

print(f"SVM Classification Report:\n{svm_report}")
```

- **Decision Trees: Making Decisions Based on Features**
  - Decision trees create a tree-like structure to make decisions based on feature values.
  - **Practical Implementation:**
- Python

```python
from sklearn.tree import DecisionTreeClassifier


# Create and train the model

tree_model = DecisionTreeClassifier()

tree_model.fit(X_train, y_train)
```

```
# Make predictions

tree_pred = tree_model.predict(X_test)


# Evaluate the model

tree_accuracy = accuracy_score(y_test, tree_pred)

tree_report = classification_report(y_test, tree_pred)


print(f"Decision Tree Accuracy: {tree_accuracy}")

print(f"Decision Tree Classification Report:\n{tree_report}")
```

- **Boosting Algorithms: Ensemble Power**
  - Boosting algorithms combine multiple weak learners to create a strong learner.
  - **Practical Implementation (Gradient Boosting):**
- Python

```
from sklearn.ensemble import GradientBoostingClassifier


# Create and train the model

boost_model = GradientBoostingClassifier()

boost_model.fit(X_train, y_train)
```

```
# Make predictions

boost_pred = boost_model.predict(X_test)


# Evaluate the model

boost_accuracy = accuracy_score(y_test, boost_pred)

boost_report = classification_report(y_test, boost_pred)


print(f"Boosting Accuracy: {boost_accuracy}")

print(f"Boosting Classification Report:\n{boost_report}")
```

-
  - **Personal Insight:** "Boosting algorithms are incredibly powerful. They can often achieve state-of-the-art results by combining the strengths of multiple weak learners. It's like having a team of experts working together to solve a problem."

Key Considerations:

- **Data Preprocessing:** Ensure your data is clean and preprocessed.
- **Feature Selection:** Select relevant features.
- **Model Evaluation:** Use appropriate metrics (accuracy, precision, recall, F1-score).

- **Hyperparameter Tuning:** Tune hyperparameters to optimize model performance.
- **Multiclass Classification:** Adapt algorithms for multiclass problems using techniques like one-vs-rest or one-vs-one.

3.3: Model Evaluation and Hyperparameter Tuning

We've built our models, but how do we know if they're any good? And how do we make them even better? This section will guide you through model evaluation techniques and hyperparameter tuning.

Model Evaluation: Measuring Performance

Model evaluation is crucial to understand how well our models perform on unseen data. Let's explore some key metrics.

- **Classification Metrics:**
  - **Accuracy:** The proportion of correctly classified instances.
  - **Precision:** The proportion of true positives among predicted positives.
  - **Recall**[2] **(Sensitivity):** The proportion of true positives among actual positives.
  - **F1-score:** The harmonic mean of precision and recall.
  - **Practical Implementation:**

from sklearn.metrics import accuracy_score, precision_score, recall_score, f1_score, classification_report

- # Assuming y_test and y_pred are already defined
- accuracy = accuracy_score(y_test, y_pred)

- precision = precision_score(y_test, y_pred)
- recall = recall_score(y_test, y_pred)
- f1 = f1_score(y_test, y_pred)
- report = classification_report(y_test, y_pred)
-
- print(f"Accuracy: {accuracy}")
- print(f"Precision: {precision}")
- print(f"Recall: {recall}")
- print(f"F1-score: {f1}")
- print(f"Classification Report:\n{report}")
- ```
- **Regression Metrics:**
  - **Mean Squared Error (MSE):** The average squared difference between predicted and actual values.
  - **Root Mean Squared Error (RMSE):** The square root of MSE.
  - **R-squared (Coefficient of Determination):** The proportion of variance in the dependent variable that is predictable from the independent variable(s).
  - **Practical Implementation:**
- Python
- from sklearn.metrics import mean_squared_error, r2_score
- import numpy as np
-
- # Assuming y_test and y_pred are already defined
- mse = mean_squared_error(y_test, y_pred)
- rmse = np.sqrt(mse)
- r2 = r2_score(y_test, y_pred)

-
- print(f"Mean Squared Error: {mse}")
- print(f"Root Mean Squared Error: {rmse}")
- print(f"R-squared: {r2}")
- **Cross-Validation:**
  - Cross-validation is a technique to assess model performance by partitioning the data into multiple folds and training/testing the model on different combinations of folds.
  - **Practical Implementation (K-Fold Cross-Validation):**

from sklearn.model_selection import cross_val_score, KFold

from sklearn.linear_model import LinearRegression

- # Assuming X and y are already defined
- model = LinearRegression()
- kf = KFold(n_splits=5, shuffle=True, random_state=42)
- scores = cross_val_score(model, X, y, cv=kf, scoring='neg_mean_squared_error')
- rmse_scores = np.sqrt(-scores)
-
- print(f"RMSE Scores: {rmse_scores}")
- print(f"Mean RMSE: {rmse_scores.mean()}")
- ```

- **Expert Commentary:** "Model evaluation is not just about getting a number; it's about understanding your model's strengths and weaknesses. Choose appropriate metrics based on your problem and use cross-validation to get a reliable estimate of performance."

Hyperparameter Tuning: Optimizing Model Performance

Hyperparameters are parameters that are set before training the model. Tuning them can significantly impact model performance.

- **Grid Search:**
  - Grid search exhaustively searches through a specified subset of the hyperparameter space.
  - **Practical Implementation:**
- Python
- from sklearn.model_selection import GridSearchCV
- from sklearn.ensemble import RandomForestClassifier
-
- # Assuming X_train, y_train, X_test, y_test are already defined
- param_grid = {
-    'n_estimators': [50, 100, 200],
-    'max_depth': [None, 10, 20],
-    'min_samples_split': [2, 5, 10]
- }
-
- model = RandomForestClassifier()
- grid_search = GridSearchCV(model, param_grid, cv=3, scoring='accuracy')
- grid_search.fit(X_train, y_train)

-
- print(f"Best Parameters: {grid_search.best_params_}")
- best_model = grid_search.best_estimator_
- y_pred = best_model.predict(X_test)
- accuracy = accuracy_score(y_test, y_pred)
- print(f"Test Accuracy with Best Parameters: {accuracy}")
- **Random Search:**
  - Random search samples a given number of candidates from a hyperparameter space with a specified distribution.
  - **Concise Explanation:** Random search is often more efficient than grid search, especially when some hyperparameters don't significantly affect performance.

Practical Implementation:

```
from sklearn.model_selection import RandomizedSearchCV

from scipy.stats import randint
```

- param_dist = {
- 'n_estimators': randint(50, 200),
- 'max_depth': [None, 10, 20, 30],
- 'min_samples_split': randint(2, 10)
- }
-

```
random_search = RandomizedSearchCV(model,
param_distributions=param_dist, n_iter=10, cv=3, scoring='accuracy',
random_state=42)
random_search.fit(X_train, y_train)

print(f"Best Parameters: {random_search.best_params_}")
```

- **Personal Insight:** "Hyperparameter tuning can feel like an art. It's about finding the right balance between exploration and exploitation. Tools like grid search and random search make the process more systematic, but domain knowledge and intuition still play a big role."

Key Considerations:

- **Validation Set:** Use a separate validation set for hyperparameter tuning to avoid overfitting.
- **Regularization:** Use regularization techniques to prevent overfitting.
- **Computational Cost:** Be mindful of the computational cost of hyperparameter tuning.

By mastering model evaluation and hyperparameter tuning, you'll be able to build high-performing AI models. Remember to choose appropriate metrics, use cross-validation, and experiment with different hyperparameter settings.

3.4: Real-World Case Studies and Applications

We've covered the theoretical aspects of supervised learning, now let's see how these algorithms are applied in the real world. This section will guide you through practical case studies and applications, showcasing the power of regression and classification.

Real-World AI Applications: From Prediction to Classification

Let's dive into some case studies that demonstrate how supervised learning algorithms are used to solve real-world problems.

- **Case Study 1: House Price Prediction (Regression)**
  - **Problem:** Predict house prices based on features like square footage, number of bedrooms, and location.
  - **Implementation:**
    - We'll use a dataset of house sales and apply linear regression or polynomial regression to predict prices.
    - **Practical Implementation:**
      -
- Python

```python
import pandas as pd

from sklearn.model_selection import train_test_split

from sklearn.linear_model import LinearRegression

from sklearn.metrics import mean_squared_error

from sklearn.preprocessing import PolynomialFeatures
```

```python
# Load the house price dataset

df = pd.read_csv("house_prices.csv")  # Replace with your dataset


# Preprocess data

X = df[['square_feet', 'bedrooms', 'bathrooms']]

y = df['price']

X_train, X_test, y_train, y_test = train_test_split(X, y, test_size=0.2,
random_state=42)


# Linear Regression

model = LinearRegression()

model.fit(X_train, y_train)

y_pred = model.predict(X_test)

mse = mean_squared_error(y_test, y_pred)

print(f"Linear Regression MSE: {mse}")


# Polynomial Regression
```

```
poly = PolynomialFeatures(degree=2)

X_poly = poly.fit_transform(X)

X_train_poly, X_test_poly, y_train, y_test = train_test_split(X_poly, y,
test_size=0.2, random_state=42)

poly_model = LinearRegression()

poly_model.fit(X_train_poly, y_train)

y_poly_pred = poly_model.predict(X_test_poly)

poly_mse = mean_squared_error(y_test, y_poly_pred)

print(f"Polynomial Regression MSE: {poly_mse}")
```

-
  - **Expert Commentary:** "House price prediction is a classic regression problem. By understanding the relationships between features and prices, we can build accurate predictive models."
- **Case Study 2: Spam Email Detection (Classification)**
  - **Problem:** Classify emails as spam or not spam based on their content and metadata.
  - **Implementation:**
    - We'll use a dataset of emails and apply logistic regression or support vector machines (SVM) to classify them.
    - **Practical Implementation:**
  -
- Python

```python
import pandas as pd

from sklearn.model_selection import train_test_split

from sklearn.linear_model import LogisticRegression

from sklearn.metrics import accuracy_score, classification_report

from sklearn.feature_extraction.text import TfidfVectorizer


# Load the spam email dataset

df = pd.read_csv("spam.csv", encoding = "latin-1") #Replace with your dataset.

df = df[["v1", "v2"]]

df = df.rename(columns = {"v1":"label", "v2":"text"})


# preprocess text

vectorizer = TfidfVectorizer()

X = vectorizer.fit_transform(df["text"])

y = df["label"].apply(lambda x: 1 if x == "spam" else 0)


# Split data
```

```
X_train, X_test, y_train, y_test = train_test_split(X, y, test_size=0.2,
random_state=42)


# Logistic Regression

model = LogisticRegression()

model.fit(X_train, y_train)

y_pred = model.predict(X_test)

accuracy = accuracy_score(y_test, y_pred)

report = classification_report(y_test, y_pred)

print(f"Logistic Regression Accuracy: {accuracy}")

print(f"Classification Report:\n{report}")
```

-
  - **Personal Insight:** "Spam email detection is a common application of classification. It's fascinating how machine learning can sift through vast amounts of text to identify patterns that indicate spam."
- **Case Study 3: Customer Churn Prediction (Classification)**
  - **Problem:** Predict which customers are likely to churn (leave) based on their behavior and demographics.
  - **Implementation:**
    - We'll use a dataset of customer data and apply decision trees or boosting algorithms to predict churn.
    - This allows businesses to take actions to retain those customers.

- **Case Study 4: Image Classification (Classification)**
  - **Problem:** Classify images into categories (e.g., cat vs. dog).
  - **Implementation:**
    - We can use Convolutional Neural Networks (CNNs) a form of deep learning, to perform image classification.[4] This is a very common use case for AI.

Key Considerations:

- **Data Quality:** Real-world datasets are often messy and require extensive preprocessing.
- **Feature Engineering:** Creating relevant features is crucial for model performance.
- **Model Selection:** Choose the appropriate algorithm based on the problem and data.
- **Evaluation:** Use appropriate metrics to evaluate model performance in the context of the problem.

These case studies demonstrate the power of supervised learning algorithms in solving real-world problems. By understanding the problem and applying the appropriate techniques, you can build effective AI solutions.

Chapter 4: Unsupervised Learning: Clustering and Dimensionality Reduction

We've explored supervised learning, where we teach machines with labeled data. Now, let's dive into unsupervised learning, where we let machines find patterns and structures in unlabeled data. Think of it as exploring a treasure map without knowing where the treasure is hidden. This chapter will cover two key techniques: clustering (grouping similar data points) and dimensionality reduction (simplifying complex data). Let's unlock some hidden insights!

4.1: Clustering Techniques: K-Means, Hierarchical Clustering

We're now stepping into the realm of unsupervised learning, where our goal is to find patterns and structures in unlabeled data. This section will guide you through two fundamental clustering techniques: K-Means and Hierarchical Clustering.

Clustering: Finding Hidden Structures

Clustering algorithms group similar data points together based on their inherent characteristics.[1] Let's explore how these techniques work.

- **K-Means Clustering: Partitioning Data into K Clusters[2]**
  - K-Means aims to partition the data into K clusters, where each data point belongs to the cluster with the nearest mean (centroid).[34]
  - **Practical Implementation:**
- Python

import pandas as pd

import numpy as np

```python
from sklearn.cluster import KMeans

import matplotlib.pyplot as plt

from sklearn.preprocessing import StandardScaler


# Sample data

data = {'X1': [1, 2, 3, 8, 9, 10], 'X2': [1, 2, 3, 8, 9, 10]}

df = pd.DataFrame(data)


# Scale the data

scaler = StandardScaler()

scaled_data = scaler.fit_transform(df)


# Apply K-Means

kmeans = KMeans(n_clusters=2, random_state=42)

df['cluster'] = kmeans.fit_predict(scaled_data)


# Visualize the clusters

plt.scatter(df['X1'], df['X2'], c=df['cluster'])
```

```python
plt.xlabel('X1')

plt.ylabel('X2')

plt.title('K-Means Clustering')

plt.show()



# Finding the optimal number of clusters (Elbow Method)

wcss = []

for i in range(1, 11):

    kmeans = KMeans(n_clusters=i, random_state=42)

    kmeans.fit(scaled_data)

    wcss.append(kmeans.inertia_)



plt.plot(range(1, 11), wcss)

plt.title('Elbow Method')

plt.xlabel('Number of clusters')

plt.ylabel('WCSS')

plt.show()
```

●

- o **Expert[5] Commentary:** "K-Means is a simple and efficient clustering algorithm, but it's sensitive to the initial centroid placement and assumes spherical clusters. The Elbow Method is a good way to find the optimal number of clusters."
- **Hierarchical Clustering: Building a Hierarchy of Clusters**
  - o Hierarchical clustering builds a hierarchy of clusters by either iteratively merging (agglomerative) or splitting (divisive) clusters.
  - o **Practical Implementation:**
- Python

```python
from sklearn.cluster import AgglomerativeClustering

from scipy.cluster.hierarchy import dendrogram, linkage


# Apply Agglomerative Clustering

agg_cluster = AgglomerativeClustering(n_clusters=2)

df['hierarchical_cluster'] = agg_cluster.fit_predict(scaled_data)


# Visualize the clusters

plt.scatter(df['X1'], df['X2'], c=df['hierarchical_cluster'])

plt.xlabel('X1')

plt.ylabel('X2')
```

```
plt.title('Hierarchical Clustering')

plt.show()


# Generate and plot the dendrogram

linked = linkage(scaled_data, 'ward')

dendrogram(linked, orientation='top', distance_sort='descending',
show_leaf_counts=True)

plt.title('Dendrogram')

plt.xlabel('Data Points')

plt.ylabel('Distance')

plt.show()
```

- **Personal Insight:** "Hierarchical clustering provides a more detailed view of the data's structure compared to K-Means. The dendrogram is a powerful tool for understanding the relationships between clusters at different levels of granularity."

Key Considerations:

- **Data Scaling:** Scaling the data is crucial for distance-based clustering algorithms.
- **Choosing the Number of Clusters:** Use techniques like the Elbow Method or silhouette score to determine the optimal number of clusters.

- **Distance Metric:** Choose an appropriate distance metric based on the data type and problem.
- **Computational Cost:** Hierarchical clustering can be computationally expensive for large datasets.

4.2: Dimensionality Reduction with PCA and Related Methods

We're now diving into dimensionality reduction, a technique that helps us handle high-dimensional data by reducing the number of features while preserving essential information.This section will guide you through Principal Component Analysis (PCA) and related methods.

Dimensionality Reduction: Simplifying Complex Data

High-dimensional data can lead to the curse of dimensionality, making models complex and inefficient.Dimensionality reduction helps us address this issue.

- **Principal Component Analysis (PCA): Transforming Data into Principal Components**
    - PCA transforms the original features into a new set of orthogonal features called principal components, which capture the maximum variance in the data.
    - **Practical Implementation:**
- Python
- import pandas as pd
- import numpy as np
- from sklearn.decomposition import PCA
- from sklearn.preprocessing import StandardScaler
- import matplotlib.pyplot as plt

```python
# Sample data
data = {'X1': [1, 2, 3, 4, 5], 'X2': [2, 3, 4, 5, 6], 'X3': [3, 4, 5, 6, 7]}
df = pd.DataFrame(data)

# Scale the data
scaler = StandardScaler()
scaled_data = scaler.fit_transform(df)

# Apply PCA
pca = PCA(n_components=2)
pca_data = pca.fit_transform(scaled_data)

# Create a DataFrame with the principal components
pca_df = pd.DataFrame(data=pca_data, columns=['PC1', 'PC2'])
print(pca_df)

# Explained variance ratio
explained_variance = pca.explained_variance_ratio_
print(f"Explained Variance Ratio: {explained_variance}")

# Visualize the transformed data
plt.scatter(pca_df['PC1'], pca_df['PC2'])
plt.xlabel('Principal Component 1')
plt.ylabel('Principal Component 2')
plt.title('PCA Transformed Data')
plt.show()
```

-
  - **Expert Commentary:** "PCA is a powerful tool for reducing dimensionality while preserving most of the data's variance.It's widely used in various applications, from image compression to feature extraction."
- **t-Distributed Stochastic Neighbor Embedding (t-SNE): Visualizing High-Dimensional Data**[7]
  - t-SNE is a non-linear dimensionality reduction technique primarily used for visualizing high-dimensional data in lower dimensions (typically 2D or 3D).
  - **Practical Implementation:**
- Python
- from sklearn.manifold import TSNE
-
- # Apply t-SNE
- tsne = TSNE(n_components=2, random_state=42)
- tsne_data = tsne.fit_transform(scaled_data)
-
- # Create a DataFrame with t-SNE components
- tsne_df = pd.DataFrame(data=tsne_data, columns=['TSNE1', 'TSNE2'])
- print(tsne_df)
-
- # Visualize the t-SNE transformed data
- plt.scatter(tsne_df['TSNE1'], tsne_df['TSNE2'])
- plt.xlabel('TSNE Component 1')
- plt.ylabel('TSNE Component 2')
- plt.title('t-SNE Transformed Data')

- plt.show()

-
  - **Personal Insight:** "t-SNE is a fantastic tool for visualizing complex datasets. It can reveal hidden structures and patterns that are difficult to see in the original high-dimensional space. However, it's important to remember that t-SNE is primarily for visualization and not for feature reduction in machine learning models."

- **UMAP (Uniform Manifold Approximation and Projection): A Modern Alternative**
  - UMAP is a modern dimensionality reduction technique that is often faster and more flexible than t-SNE.
  - **Practical Implementation:**
- Python
- import umap
-
- # Apply UMAP
- reducer = umap.UMAP(n_components=2, random_state=42)
- umap_data = reducer.fit_transform(scaled_data)
-
- # Create a DataFrame with UMAP components
- umap_df = pd.DataFrame(data=umap_data, columns=['UMAP1', 'UMAP2'])
- print(umap_df)
-
- # Visualize the UMAP transformed data
- plt.scatter(umap_df['UMAP1'], umap_df['UMAP2'])
- plt.xlabel('UMAP Component 1')
- plt.ylabel('UMAP Component 2')

- plt.title('UMAP Transformed Data')
- plt.show()
-
    - ○ **Concise Explanation:** UMAP is good at preserving both local and global structure of data, and can be used for both visualization and feature reduction.

Key Considerations:

- **Data Scaling:** Scaling the data is crucial for PCA and related methods.
- **Choosing the Number of Components:** Use techniques like explained variance ratio or visual inspection to determine the optimal number of components.
- **Computational Cost:** t-SNE can be computationally expensive for large datasets.
- **Interpretability:** PCA provides interpretable components, while t-SNE and UMAP are less interpretable.

4.3: Applications in Data Visualization and Anomaly Detection

We've explored clustering and dimensionality reduction, and now we'll see how these techniques are applied in two crucial areas: data visualization and anomaly detection.

Unsupervised Learning in Action: Visualizing and Detecting Anomalies

Unsupervised learning algorithms are powerful tools for gaining insights into unlabeled data. Let's see how they're used in practice.

- **Data Visualization: Unveiling Hidden Patterns**
  - Dimensionality reduction techniques like t-SNE and UMAP are invaluable for visualizing high-dimensional data in lower dimensions.
  - **Practical Implementation (Visualizing MNIST Digits):**
    - Python

```python
import numpy as np

import matplotlib.pyplot as plt

from sklearn.datasets import load_digits

from sklearn.manifold import TSNE

import umap


# Load the MNIST digits dataset

digits = load_digits()

data = digits.data

labels = digits.target


# Apply t-SNE for visualization

tsne = TSNE(n_components=2, random_state=42)

tsne_data = tsne.fit_transform(data)
```

```
# Plot the t-SNE visualization

plt.scatter(tsne_data[:, 0], tsne_data[:, 1], c=labels, cmap='viridis')

plt.colorbar(label='Digit Label')

plt.title('t-SNE Visualization of MNIST Digits')

plt.show()



# Apply UMAP for visualization

reducer = umap.UMAP(n_components=2, random_state=42)

umap_data = reducer.fit_transform(data)



# Plot the UMAP visualization

plt.scatter(umap_data[:, 0], umap_data[:, 1], c=labels, cmap='viridis')

plt.colorbar(label='Digit Label')

plt.title('UMAP Visualization of MNIST Digits')

plt.show()
```

- o **Expert Commentary:** "Visualizing high-dimensional data with
  t-SNE or UMAP can reveal clusters and patterns that are not apparent

in the original data. This is crucial for exploratory data analysis and gaining insights into complex datasets."

- **Anomaly Detection: Identifying Unusual Data Points**
  - ○ Clustering and dimensionality reduction can be used to identify anomalies or outliers in data.
  - ○ **Practical Implementation (Anomaly Detection with Isolation Forest):**
    - Python

```
import pandas as pd

from sklearn.ensemble import IsolationForest

import matplotlib.pyplot as plt


# Sample data with anomalies

data = {'X1': [1, 2, 3, 4, 5, 100], 'X2': [1, 2, 3, 4, 5, 200]}

df = pd.DataFrame(data)


# Apply Isolation Forest

iso_forest = IsolationForest(contamination=0.1, random_state=42)

df['anomaly'] = iso_forest.fit_predict(df[['X1', 'X2']])
```

```python
# Visualize the anomalies

anomalies = df[df['anomaly'] == -1]

normal_data = df[df['anomaly'] == 1]


plt.scatter(normal_data['X1'], normal_data['X2'], label='Normal')

plt.scatter(anomalies['X1'], anomalies['X2'], color='red', label='Anomaly')

plt.xlabel('X1')

plt.ylabel('X2')

plt.title('Anomaly Detection with Isolation Forest')

plt.legend()

plt.show()
```

- o **Personal Insight:** "Anomaly detection is a critical application of unsupervised learning. It helps us identify unusual patterns in data, which can be indicative of fraud, errors, or other important events. Isolation Forest is a powerful and efficient algorithm for this task."
- **Anomaly Detection with Clustering:**
  - o You can use clustering, to identify data points that do not fall into any well-defined cluster.
  - o Points far from cluster centroids can be marked as anomalies.
- **Anomaly Detection with PCA:**

- PCA can be used to identify anomalies by looking at the reconstruction error.High reconstruction error indicates an anomaly.

Key Considerations:

- **Data Preprocessing:** Ensure your data is clean and scaled before applying these techniques.

- **Algorithm Selection:** Choose the appropriate algorithm based on the data and problem.

- **Parameter Tuning:** Tune the parameters of the algorithms to optimize performance.

- **Interpretation:** Understand the results and interpret them in the context of the problem.

You've now seen how unsupervised learning techniques are used in data visualization and anomaly detection. By understanding these applications, you can leverage unsupervised learning to gain valuable insights from your data.

Chapter 5: Deep Learning with TensorFlow and Keras

We've journeyed through traditional machine learning, and now it's time to explore the fascinating world of deep learning. Think of deep learning as giving our machines a much more powerful brain, capable of tackling complex tasks like image recognition and language processing. In this chapter, we'll dive into building neural networks with TensorFlow and Keras. Let's build some deep models!

5.1: Building Neural Networks with Keras

We're now stepping into the realm of deep learning, and Keras is our construction toolkit. This section will guide you through building neural networks using Keras, a high-level API that makes deep learning accessible and intuitive.

Keras: Your Deep Learning Construction Kit

Keras simplifies the process of building and training neural networks. Let's get started with some practical examples.

- **Building a Simple Neural Network for Classification:**
  - We'll create a basic neural network for a binary classification problem.
  - **Practical Implementation:**
- Python

```
import numpy as np

import tensorflow as tf

from tensorflow import keras
```

```python
from sklearn.model_selection import train_test_split

from sklearn.preprocessing import StandardScaler


# Sample data

data = np.array([[1, 2], [2, 3], [3, 4], [8, 9], [9, 10], [10, 11]])

labels = np.array([0, 0, 0, 1, 1, 1])


# Scale the data

scaler = StandardScaler()

scaled_data = scaler.fit_transform(data)


# Split data

X_train, X_test, y_train, y_test = train_test_split(scaled_data, labels, test_size=0.2,
random_state=42)


# Build the model

model = keras.Sequential([

    keras.layers.Dense(12, activation='relu', input_shape=(2,)),
```

```python
    keras.layers.Dense(1, activation='sigmoid')

])


# Compile the model

model.compile(optimizer='adam', loss='binary_crossentropy', metrics=['accuracy'])


# Train the model

model.fit(X_train, y_train, epochs=50, batch_size=2, validation_split=0.1)


# Evaluate the model

loss, accuracy = model.evaluate(X_test, y_test)

print(f"Test Loss: {loss}, Test Accuracy: {accuracy}")
```

-
  - **Expert Commentary:** "Keras's Sequential model makes it easy to build simple neural networks layer by layer. The 'relu' activation function is commonly used for hidden layers, and 'sigmoid' for binary classification output."
- **Building a Convolutional Neural Network (CNN) for Image Classification:**
  - We'll create a CNN for image classification using the MNIST dataset.
  - **Practical Implementation:**

```python
from tensorflow.keras.datasets import mnist

from tensorflow.keras.models import Sequential

from tensorflow.keras.layers1 import Conv2D, MaxPooling2D, Flatten, Dense

from tensorflow.keras.utils import to_categorical2

# Load the MNIST dataset

(X_train, y_train), (X_test, y_test) = mnist.load_data()


# Preprocess the data

X_train = X_train.reshape((60000, 28, 28, 1)).astype('float32') / 255

X_test = X_test.reshape((10000, 28, 28, 1)).astype('float32') / 255

y_train = to_categorical(y_train)

y_test = to_categorical(y_test)


# Build the CNN model

cnn_model = Sequential([

    Conv2D(32, (3, 3), activation='relu', input_shape=(28, 28, 1)),

    MaxPooling2D((2, 2)),

    Conv2D(64, (3, 3), activation='relu'),
```

```python
    MaxPooling2D((2, 2)),

    Flatten(),

    Dense(128, activation='relu'),

    Dense(10, activation='softmax')

])


# Compile the model

cnn_model.compile(optimizer='adam', loss='categorical_crossentropy',
metrics=['accuracy'])


# Train the model

cnn_model.fit(X_train, y_train, epochs=5, batch_size=64, validation_split=0.1)


# Evaluate the model

loss, accuracy = cnn_model.evaluate(X_test, y_test)

print(f"CNN Test Loss: {loss}, CNN Test Accuracy: {accuracy}")

```

"Building CNNs with Keras is incredibly intuitive. The Conv2D and MaxPooling2D layers make it easy to extract features from images, and the Flatten and Dense layers allow us to make predictions based on those features."

- **Building a Recurrent Neural Network (RNN) for Sequence Prediction:**
  - We'll create an RNN for a simple sequence prediction task.
- Python

```
from tensorflow.keras.layers import LSTM


# Sample sequence data

sequence_data = np.array([[[0.1, 0.2, 0.3], [0.2, 0.3, 0.4], [0.3, 0.4, 0.5]],

                [[0.4, 0.5, 0.6], [0.5, 0.6, 0.7], [0.6, 0.7, 0.8]]])

sequence_labels = np.array([[0.4, 0.5, 0.6], [0.7, 0.8, 0.9]])


# Build the RNN model

rnn_model = Sequential([

    LSTM(50, activation='relu', input_shape=(3, 3)),

    Dense(3)

])
```

```python
# Compile the model

rnn_model.compile(optimizer='adam', loss='mse')


# Train the model

rnn_model.fit(sequence_data, sequence_labels, epochs=100, verbose=0)


# Make predictions

predictions = rnn_model.predict(sequence_data)

print(predictions)
```

Key Considerations:

- **Activation Functions:** Choose appropriate activation functions for your layers.
- **Loss Functions:** Select a loss function that matches your problem type.
- **Optimizers:** Experiment with different optimizers to improve convergence.
- **Hyperparameter Tuning:** Tune hyperparameters (e.g., number of layers, neurons, epochs) to optimize model performance.
- **Data Preprocessing:** Ensure your data is properly preprocessed before training.

5.2: Convolutional Neural Networks (CNNs) for Image Analysis

Let's dive deeper into deep learning, focusing on Convolutional Neural Networks (CNNs), the workhorses of image analysis. This section will guide you through building and understanding CNNs for various image-related tasks.

CNNs: The Visionaries of Deep Learning

CNNs excel at processing grid-like data, such as images. Their unique architecture allows them to learn hierarchical features, making them highly effective for image classification, object detection, and more.

- **Understanding CNN Architecture:**
    - **Convolutional Layers (Conv2D):** Extract features by applying filters to the input image.
    - **Pooling Layers (MaxPooling2D):** Reduce the spatial dimensions of feature maps, reducing computational load and making the model more robust to variations.
    - **Flatten Layer:** Converts the multi-dimensional feature maps into a one-dimensional vector.
    - **Dense Layers:** Fully connected layers for final classification or regression.
    - **Practical Implementation (Building a Basic CNN):**
- Python
- import tensorflow as tf
- from tensorflow.keras.models import Sequential
- from tensorflow.keras.layers import Conv2D, MaxPooling2D, Flatten, Dense

```python
from tensorflow.keras.datasets import cifar10
from tensorflow.keras.utils import to_categorical

# Load the CIFAR-10 dataset
(X_train, y_train), (X_test, y_test) = cifar10.load_data()

# Preprocess the data
X_train = X_train.astype('float32') / 255
X_test = X_test.astype('float32') / 255
y_train = to_categorical(y_train)
y_test = to_categorical(y_test)

# Build the CNN model
cnn_model = Sequential([
    Conv2D(32, (3, 3), activation='relu', input_shape=(32, 32, 3)),
    MaxPooling2D((2, 2)),
    Conv2D(64, (3, 3), activation='relu'),
    MaxPooling2D((2, 2)),
    Flatten(),
    Dense(128, activation='relu'),
    Dense(10, activation='softmax')
])

# Compile the model
cnn_model.compile(optimizer='adam', loss='categorical_crossentropy',
    metrics=['accuracy'])
```

- # Train the model
- cnn_model.fit(X_train, y_train, epochs=10, batch_size=64, validation_split=0.1)
-
- # Evaluate the model
- loss, accuracy = cnn_model.evaluate(X_test, y_test)
- print(f"CNN Test Loss: {loss}, CNN Test Accuracy: {accuracy}")
-
  - **Expert Commentary:** "CNNs are designed to automatically learn spatial hierarchies of features from images. Convolutional layers act as feature detectors, while pooling layers reduce dimensionality and increase robustness."
- **Data Augmentation: Improving Generalization**
  - Data augmentation techniques artificially increase the size of the training dataset by applying transformations to the images.

Practical Implementation:

from tensorflow.keras.preprocessing.image import ImageDataGenerator

- # Create an ImageDataGenerator for data augmentation
- datagen = ImageDataGenerator(
- rotation_range=20,
- width_shift_range=0.2,
- height_shift_range=0.2,
- horizontal_flip=True
-)

-
- # Train the model with augmented data
- datagen.fit(X_train)
- cnn_model.fit(datagen.flow(X_train, y_train, batch_size=64), epochs=10, validation_data=(X_test, y_test))
- ```
-
- Personal Insight:"Data augmentation is a game-changer for image classification. It allows us to train robust models with limited data by introducing variations in the training set. It also helps to prevent overfitting."
- **Transfer Learning: Leveraging Pre-trained Models**
  - Transfer learning involves using pre-trained models (e.g., VGG16, ResNet) as a starting point for new tasks.
  - **Practical Implementation (Using VGG16):**
- Python
- from tensorflow.keras.applications import VGG16
- from tensorflow.keras.layers import GlobalAveragePooling2D
- from tensorflow.keras.models import Model
-
- # Load the pre-trained VGG16 model (without top layers)
- base_model = VGG16(weights='imagenet', include_top=False, input_shape=(32, 32, 3))
-
- # Freeze the base model layers
- base_model.trainable = False
-
- # Add custom classification layers

- x = base_model.output
- x = GlobalAveragePooling2D()(x)
- x = Dense(128, activation='relu')(x)
- predictions = Dense(10, activation='softmax')(x)
-
- # Create the final model
- transfer_model = Model(inputs=base_model.input, outputs=predictions)
-
- # Compile and train the model
- transfer_model.compile(optimizer='adam', loss='categorical_crossentropy', metrics=['accuracy'])
- transfer_model.fit(X_train, y_train, epochs=5, batch_size=64, validation_data=(X_test, y_test))
-
  - **Concise Explanation:** Transfer learning allows us to leverage the knowledge learned by pre-trained models on large datasets, significantly reducing training time and improving performance on new tasks.

Key Considerations:

- **Input Shape:** Ensure your input images have the correct shape for the CNN.
- **Convolutional Filters:** Experiment with different filter sizes and numbers.
- **Pooling Layers:** Choose appropriate pooling strategies.
- **Activation Functions:** Use ReLU for hidden layers and softmax for multi-class classification.
- **Regularization:** Use techniques like dropout to prevent overfitting.

5.3: Recurrent Neural Networks (RNNs) for Sequence Data

We're now delving into Recurrent Neural Networks (RNNs), the masters of sequence data. This section will guide you through building and understanding RNNs for tasks like time series analysis, natural language processing, and more.

RNNs: The Memory Keepers of Deep Learning

RNNs are designed to process sequential data by maintaining a hidden state that captures information from previous time steps.This allows them to model dependencies and patterns in sequences.

- **Understanding RNN Architecture:**
  - **Recurrent Layers (SimpleRNN, LSTM, GRU):** Process sequences by iterating through time steps and updating a hidden state.
  - **Time Distributed Layers:** Apply a layer to every time step of the input sequence.
  - **Embedding Layers:** Convert categorical inputs into dense vectors.

Practical Implementation (Building a Simple RNN):

import numpy as np

import tensorflow as tf

from tensorflow.keras.models import Sequential

from tensorflow.keras.layers7 import SimpleRNN, Dense8

- # Sample sequence data (time steps, features)

```
data = np.array([[[0.1, 0.2, 0.3], [0.2, 0.3, 0.4], [0.3, 0.4, 0.5]],
        [[0.4, 0.5, 0.6], [0.5, 0.6, 0.7], [0.6, 0.7, 0.8]]])
labels = np.array([[0.4, 0.5, 0.6], [0.7, 0.8, 0.9]])

# Build the RNN model
rnn_model = Sequential([
    SimpleRNN(50, activation='relu', input_shape=(3, 3)),
    Dense(3)
])

# Compile the model
rnn_model.compile(optimizer='adam', loss='mse')

# Train the model
rnn_model.fit(data, labels, epochs=200, verbose=0)

# Make predictions
predictions = rnn_model.predict(data)
print(predictions)
```

Expert Commentary:"RNNs are designed to handle sequential data by maintaining a memory of past inputs. However, simple RNNs can suffer from vanishing or exploding gradients, making it difficult to learn long-range dependencies."

- **Long Short-Term Memory (LSTM) and Gated Recurrent Unit (GRU): Addressing Long-Term Dependencies:**
  - LSTMs and GRUs are specialized RNN architectures that use gating mechanisms to control the flow of information and mitigate the vanishing gradient problem.
  -
  - **Practical Implementation (Building an LSTM):**
- Python
- from tensorflow.keras.layers import LSTM
-
- # Build the LSTM model
- lstm_model = Sequential([
-    LSTM(50, activation='relu', input_shape=(3, 3)),
-    Dense(3)
-])
-
- # Compile and train the model
- lstm_model.compile(optimizer='adam', loss='mse')
- lstm_model.fit(data, labels, epochs=200, verbose=0)
-
- # Make predictions
- lstm_predictions = lstm_model.predict(data)
- print(lstm_predictions)
-
-
  - **Personal Insight:** "LSTMs and GRUs are game-changers for sequence modeling. They allow RNNs to learn long-range

dependencies, making them suitable for tasks like natural language processing and time series forecasting. GRUs are often preferred for their computational efficiency."

- **Embedding Layers and Text Processing:**
  - Embedding layers convert words or tokens into dense vectors, capturing semantic relationships.
  - **Practical Implementation (Text Generation with LSTM):**
- Python
- from tensorflow.keras.layers import Embedding
- from tensorflow.keras.utils import to_categorical
-
- # Sample text data
- text = "the quick brown fox jumps over the lazy dog"
- tokens = text.split()
- vocab_size = len(set(tokens))
- word_to_index = {word: i for i, word in enumerate(set(tokens))}
- sequences = [word_to_index[word] for word in tokens]
- sequences = np.array(sequences)
- sequences_one_hot = to_categorical(sequences)
-
- # Build the LSTM model with Embedding
- embedding_model = Sequential([
-     Embedding(vocab_size, 10, input_length=len(sequences)),
-     LSTM(50, activation='relu'),
-     Dense(vocab_size, activation='softmax')
-])
-

- # Compile and train the model
- embedding_model.compile(optimizer='adam', loss='categorical_crossentropy')
- embedding_model.fit(np.array([sequences]), np.array([sequences_one_hot]), epochs=200, verbose=0)
-
- # Generate text
- seed_text = "the quick brown"
- seed_tokens = seed_text.split()
- seed_sequence = [word_to_index[word] for word in seed_tokens]
- seed_sequence = np.array([seed_sequence])
-
- predicted_index = np.argmax(embedding_model.predict(seed_sequence))
- predicted_word = list(word_to_index.keys())[list(word_to_index.values()).index(predicted_index)]
- print(f"{seed_text} {predicted_word}")

Key Considerations:

- **Sequence Length:** Handle variable-length sequences using padding or masking.
- **Recurrent Architecture:** Choose appropriate recurrent layers (LSTM, GRU) based on the task.
- **Embedding Layers:** Use embedding layers for categorical sequence data.
- **Time Distributed Layers:** Apply layers to each time step for sequence-to-sequence tasks.

- **Bidirectional RNNs:** Use bidirectional RNNs to capture dependencies from both past and future time steps.

5.4: Practical Image and Time-Series Projects

We've covered the theoretical aspects of CNNs and RNNs, now let's apply our knowledge to some practical projects. This section will guide you through building real-world applications using these powerful deep learning architectures.

Deep Learning in Action: Image and Time-Series Projects

Let's dive into some projects that demonstrate the practical applications of CNNs and RNNs.

- **Project 1: Image Classification with CNNs (Cat vs. Dog)**
  - **Problem:** Build a CNN to classify images of cats and dogs.
  - **Implementation:**
    - We'll use a dataset of cat and dog images and apply a CNN to classify them.
    - **Practical Implementation:**
- Python

```
import tensorflow as tf

from tensorflow.keras.models import Sequential

from tensorflow.keras.layers import Conv2D, MaxPooling2D, Flatten, Dense

from tensorflow.keras.preprocessing.image import ImageDataGenerator
```

```python
# Data preprocessing

train_datagen = ImageDataGenerator(rescale=1./255,

                    shear_range=0.2,

                    zoom_range=0.2,

                    horizontal_flip=True)

test_datagen = ImageDataGenerator(rescale=1./255)


training_set = train_datagen.flow_from_directory('dataset/training_set',

                    target_size=(64, 64),

                    batch_size=32,

                    class_mode='binary')


test_set = test_datagen.flow_from_directory('dataset/test_set',

                    target_size=(64, 64),

                    batch_size=32,

                    class_mode='binary')


# Building the CNN
```

```python
cnn = Sequential()

cnn.add(Conv2D(32, (3, 3), activation='relu', input_shape=(64, 64, 3)))

cnn.add(MaxPooling2D((2, 2)))

cnn.add(Conv2D(64, (3, 3), activation='relu'))

cnn.add(MaxPooling2D((2, 2)))

cnn.add(Flatten())

cnn.add(Dense(units=128, activation='relu'))

cnn.add(Dense(units=1, activation='sigmoid'))


# Compiling and training the CNN

cnn.compile(optimizer='adam', loss='binary_crossentropy', metrics=['accuracy'])

cnn.fit(x=training_set, validation_data=test_set, epochs=25)
```

-
  - **Expert Commentary:** "This project demonstrates the power of CNNs for image classification. Data augmentation is crucial for improving model generalization with limited training data."
- **Project 2: Time Series Forecasting with RNNs (Stock Price Prediction)**
  - **Problem:** Build an RNN to predict future stock prices based on historical data.

- ○ **Implementation:**
  - ■ We'll use a dataset of stock prices and apply an LSTM to forecast future values.
  - ■ **Practical Implementation:**
    - ○
- Python

```python
import numpy as np

import pandas as pd

import tensorflow as tf

from tensorflow.keras.models import Sequential

from tensorflow.keras.layers import LSTM, Dense

from sklearn.preprocessing import MinMaxScaler


# Load the stock price dataset

df = pd.read_csv('stock_prices.csv')  # Replace with your dataset


# Preprocess the data

scaler = MinMaxScaler(feature_range=(0, 1))
```

```python
scaled_data = scaler.fit_transform(df['Close'].values.reshape(-1, 1))


# Create sequences

def create_sequences(data, seq_length):

    xs, ys = [], []

    for i in range(len(data) - seq_length):

        x = data[i:i + seq_length]

        y = data[i + seq_length]

        xs.append(x)

        ys.append(y)

    return np.array(xs), np.array(ys)


seq_length = 60

X, y = create_sequences(scaled_data, seq_length)


# Split data

split = int(0.8 * len(X))

X_train, y_train, X_test, y_test = X[:split], y[:split], X[split:], y[split:]
```

```
# Build the LSTM model

lstm_model = Sequential([

    LSTM(units=50, return_sequences=True, input_shape=(X_train.shape[1], 1)),

    LSTM(units=50),

    Dense(units=1)

])



# Compile and train the model

lstm_model.compile(optimizer='adam', loss='mean_squared_error')

lstm_model.fit(X_train, y_train, epochs=100, batch_size=32)



# Make predictions

predictions = lstm_model.predict(X_test)

predictions = scaler.inverse_transform(predictions)
```

- o **Personal Insight:** "Time series forecasting with RNNs is a challenging but rewarding task. LSTMs can capture complex temporal dependencies, making them suitable for predicting stock prices and other time-dependent data."

- **Project 3: Image Generation with GANs.**
  - Generative Adversarial Networks are powerful tools for generating new images.
  - This project will create a network that can generate images of hand written digits.
- **Project 4: Text Generation with LSTMs.**
  - LSTMs can be used to generate text.
  - This project will create a network that can generate text in the style of a chosen author.

Key Considerations:

- **Data Preprocessing:** Ensure your data is properly preprocessed for CNNs and RNNs.
- **Model Architecture:** Choose appropriate architectures based on the problem.
- **Hyperparameter Tuning:** Tune hyperparameters to optimize model performance.
- **Evaluation:** Use appropriate metrics to evaluate model performance.

Chapter 6: Deep Learning with PyTorch

Now it's time to explore another powerful deep learning framework: PyTorch. Think of PyTorch as a more flexible and dynamic tool, especially loved by researchers and those who like to build custom models. In this chapter, we'll learn the basics of PyTorch and build neural networks for various tasks. Let's get our hands on some tensors!

6.1: PyTorch Fundamentals and Tensor Operations

We're now diving into the world of PyTorch, a powerful and flexible deep learning framework. This section will guide you through the fundamentals of PyTorch, focusing on tensor operations and the dynamic computation graph.

PyTorch: Your Dynamic Deep Learning Playground

PyTorch is known for its dynamic computation graph, which allows for greater flexibility and ease of debugging compared to static graph frameworks. Let's get started with some practical examples.

- **Tensors: The Building Blocks of PyTorch**
    - Tensors are multi-dimensional arrays, similar to NumPy arrays, but with GPU acceleration capabilities.
    - **Practical Implementation:**
- Python

```
import torch

import numpy as np
```

```python
# Creating tensors

tensor_from_list = torch.tensor([1, 2, 3])

tensor_from_numpy = torch.from_numpy(np.array([4, 5, 6]))

zeros_tensor = torch.zeros(2, 3)

ones_tensor = torch.ones(2, 3)

random_tensor = torch.rand(2, 3)


print("Tensor from list:", tensor_from_list)

print("Tensor from NumPy:", tensor_from_numpy)

print("Zeros tensor:", zeros_tensor)

print("Ones tensor:", ones_tensor)

print("Random tensor:", random_tensor)


# Tensor operations

tensor_a = torch.tensor([1, 2, 3])

tensor_b = torch.tensor([4, 5, 6])


addition = tensor_a + tensor_b
```

```python
multiplication = tensor_a * tensor_b

dot_product = torch.dot(tensor_a, tensor_b)


print("Addition:", addition)

print("Multiplication:", multiplication)

print("Dot product:", dot_product)


# GPU acceleration

if torch.cuda.is_available():

    device = torch.device('cuda')

    gpu_tensor = torch.tensor([7, 8, 9]).to(device)

    print("GPU Tensor:", gpu_tensor)

else:

    print("CUDA is not available. Running on CPU.")
```

- **Expert Commentary:** "Tensors are the fundamental data structure in PyTorch. They're similar to NumPy arrays, but with the added benefit of GPU acceleration, which is crucial for deep learning."
- **Autograd: Automatic Differentiation**
  - PyTorch's autograd system automatically computes gradients, which are essential for training neural networks.

- ○ **Practical Implementation:**
  - Python

```
x = torch.tensor(2.0, requires_grad=True)

y = x**2 + 2*x + 1



y.backward()  # Compute gradients



print("Gradient of y with respect to x:", x.grad)
```

-
  - ○ **Personal Insight:** "Autograd is one of PyTorch's killer features. It simplifies the process of computing gradients, allowing us to focus on building and training neural networks without worrying about manual differentiation."
- **Dynamic Computation Graph:**
  - ○ PyTorch builds the computation graph dynamically, which allows for greater flexibility and ease of debugging.
  - ○ **Concise Explanation:** In static graph frameworks, the computation graph is defined before execution, while in PyTorch, it's defined on-the-fly. This allows for more intuitive debugging and control flow.
- **Tensor Operations and Manipulation:**
  - ○ PyTorch provides a wide range of tensor operations for reshaping, slicing, and manipulating tensors.

- ○ **Practical Implementation:**
- Python

```python
tensor = torch.arange(12).reshape(3, 4)

print("Original Tensor:", tensor)


reshaped_tensor = tensor.view(4, 3)

print("Reshaped Tensor:", reshaped_tensor)


sliced_tensor = tensor[:, 1:3]

print("Sliced Tensor:", sliced_tensor)


concatenated_tensor = torch.cat((tensor, tensor), dim=0)

print("Concatenated Tensor:", concatenated_tensor)
```

Key Considerations:

- **GPU Acceleration:** Leverage GPU acceleration for faster training.
- **Autograd:** Use autograd to automatically compute gradients.
- **Tensor Operations:** Familiarize yourself with PyTorch's tensor operations for efficient data manipulation.
- **Dynamic Graph:** Understand the dynamic computation graph for effective debugging.

You've now learned the fundamentals of PyTorch tensors and autograd. Remember to leverage GPU acceleration, use autograd for automatic differentiation, and familiarize yourself with PyTorch's tensor operations. Let's move on to building neural networks with PyTorch.

6.2: Building Custom Neural Network Architectures in PyTorch

Let's move beyond simple models and diving into building custom neural network architectures. This section will guide you through creating complex and tailored models using PyTorch's nn.Module class.

PyTorch's nn.Module: Your Architecture Blueprint

PyTorch's nn.Module class is the foundation for building custom neural networks. It allows you to define your model's layers and forward pass, giving you complete control over your architecture.

- **Defining Custom Modules:**
  - We'll create a custom module for a simple feedforward neural network.
  - **Practical Implementation:**
- Python
  - import torch
  - import torch.nn as nn
  - import torch.nn.functional as F
  -
  - class SimpleNet(nn.Module):
  -     def __init__(self, input_size, hidden_size, output_size):
  -         super(SimpleNet, self).__init__()

```python
        self.fc1 = nn.Linear(input_size, hidden_size)
        self.fc2 = nn.Linear(hidden_size, output_size)

    def forward(self, x):
        x = F.relu(self.fc1(x))
        x = self.fc2(x)
        return x

# Instantiate the model
input_size = 10
hidden_size = 20
output_size = 5
model = SimpleNet(input_size, hidden_size, output_size)

# Sample input
input_tensor = torch.randn(1, input_size)

# Forward pass
output_tensor = model(input_tensor)
print("Output Tensor:", output_tensor)
```

-
  - **Expert Commentary:** "Defining custom modules with nn.Module allows you to create complex and tailored neural network architectures. The forward method defines the flow of data through the network."
- **Building Complex Architectures:**

- We'll create a more complex architecture with multiple layers and custom operations.
- **Practical Implementation:**

- Python

```python
class ComplexNet(nn.Module):
    def __init__(self, input_size, hidden_sizes, output_size):
        super(ComplexNet, self).__init__()
        self.layers = nn.ModuleList()
        layer_sizes = [input_size] + hidden_sizes
        for i in range(len(layer_sizes) - 1):
            self.layers.append(nn.Linear(layer_sizes[i], layer_sizes[i+1]))
        self.output_layer = nn.Linear(hidden_sizes[-1], output_size)

    def forward(self, x):
        for layer in self.layers:
            x = F.relu(layer(x))
        x = self.output_layer(x)
        return x

# Instantiate the complex model
input_size = 10
hidden_sizes = [20, 30, 20]
output_size = 5
complex_model = ComplexNet(input_size, hidden_sizes, output_size)

# Sample input
input_tensor = torch.randn(1, input_size)
```

- ○
- ○ # Forward pass
- ○ output_tensor = complex_model(input_tensor)
- ○ print("Complex Output Tensor:", output_tensor)
- ○ **Personal Insight:** "Using nn.ModuleList allows you to dynamically create and manage layers in your model. This is particularly useful for building architectures with varying numbers of layers or custom operations."

- **Custom Layers and Operations:**
  - ○ You can create custom layers by inheriting from nn.Module and defining your own forward pass.
  - ○ **Concise Explanation:** This allows you to implement specialized operations or non-standard layers that are not available in the built-in PyTorch modules.

- **Using Pre-trained Models as Building Blocks:**
  - ○ You can integrate pre-trained models (e.g., ResNet, VGG) into your custom architectures.
  - ○ **Practical Implementation:**

- Python
  - ○ import torchvision.models as models
  - ○
  - ○ class TransferModel(nn.Module):
  - ○   def __init__(self, num_classes):
  - ○   super(TransferModel, self).__init__()
  - ○   self.resnet = models.resnet18(pretrained=True)
  - ○   self.resnet.fc = nn.Linear(self.resnet.fc.in_features, num_classes)
  - ○

```
o    def forward(self, x):

o        return self.resnet(x)

o

o    # Instantiate the transfer model

o    num_classes = 10

o    transfer_model = TransferModel(num_classes)

o

o    # Sample input

o    input_tensor = torch.randn(1, 3, 224, 224) # ResNet expects 3 channel
     images of size 224x224.

o

o    # Forward pass

o    output_tensor = transfer_model(input_tensor)

o    print("Transfer Output Tensor:", output_tensor).
```

Key Considerations:

- **Inheritance:** Inherit from nn.Module to create custom modules.
- __init__ **and** forward**:** Define layers in __init__ and the forward pass in forward.
- nn.ModuleList: Use nn.ModuleList to manage dynamic layers.
- **Pre-trained Models:** Leverage pre-trained models for transfer learning.
- **Custom Layers:** Create custom layers for specialized operations.

You've now learned how to build custom neural network architectures in PyTorch. Remember to use nn.Module for defining your models, nn.ModuleList for dynamic layers, and leverage pre-trained models for transfer learning. Let's move on to training and optimizing PyTorch models.

6.3: CNNs and RNNs with PyTorch

We're now applying our PyTorch fundamentals to build Convolutional Neural Networks (CNNs) and Recurrent Neural Networks (RNNs). This section will guide you through creating and training these powerful architectures using PyTorch.

CNNs and RNNs in PyTorch: Power and Flexibility

PyTorch's dynamic computation graph and intuitive API make it ideal for building and experimenting with CNNs and RNNs. Let's dive into some practical examples.

- **Building a CNN for Image Classification:**
    - We'll create a CNN for image classification using the CIFAR-10 dataset.
    - **Practical Implementation:**
- Python
- import torch
- import torch.nn as nn
- import torch.nn.functional as F
- import torchvision
- import torchvision.transforms as transforms
- import torch.optim as optim
-
- # Data loading and preprocessing
- transform = transforms.Compose([transforms.ToTensor(), transforms.Normalize((0.5, 0.5, 0.5), (0.5, 0.5, 0.5))])

- trainset = torchvision.datasets.CIFAR10(root='./data', train=True, download=True, transform=transform)
- trainloader = torch.utils.data.DataLoader(trainset, batch_size=4, shuffle=True, num_workers=2)
- testset = torchvision.datasets.CIFAR10(root='./data', train=False, download=True, transform=transform)
- testloader = torch.utils.data.DataLoader(testset, batch_size=4, shuffle=False, num_workers=2)
- classes = ('plane', 'car', 'bird', 'cat', 'deer', 'dog', 'frog', 'horse', 'ship', 'truck')
-
- # Define the CNN architecture
- class Net(nn.Module):
-   def __init__(self):
-     super(Net, self).__init__()
-     self.conv1 = nn.Conv2D(3, 6, 5)
-     self.pool = nn.MaxPool2D(2, 2)
-     self.conv2 = nn.Conv2D(6, 16, 5)
-     self.fc1 = nn.Linear(16 * 5 * 5, 120)
-     self.fc2 = nn.Linear(120, 84)
-     self.fc3 = nn.Linear(84, 10)
-
-   def forward(self, x):
-     x = self.pool(F.relu(self.conv1(x)))
-     x = self.pool(F.relu(self.conv2(x)))
-     x = x.view(-1, 16 * 5 * 5)
-     x = F.relu(self.fc1(x))
-     x = F.relu(self.fc2(x))

```python
        x = self.fc3(x)
        return x

net = Net()

# Define loss function and optimizer
criterion = nn.CrossEntropyLoss()
optimizer = optim.SGD(net.parameters(), lr=0.001, momentum=0.9)

# Train the CNN
for epoch in range(2):  # loop over the dataset multiple times
    for i, data in enumerate(trainloader, 0):
        inputs, labels = data
        optimizer.zero_grad()
        outputs = net(inputs)
        loss = criterion(outputs, labels)
        loss.backward()
        optimizer.step()

print('Finished Training')

# Evaluate the CNN
correct = 0
total = 0
with torch.no_grad():
    for data in testloader:
        images, labels = data
```

- outputs = net(images)
- _, predicted = torch.max(outputs.data, 1)
- total += labels.size(0)
- correct += (predicted == labels).sum().item()
-
- print(f'Accuracy of the network on the 10000 test images: {100 * correct / total} %')
-
  - **Expert[1] Commentary:** "PyTorch's nn.Conv2D and nn.MaxPool2D layers make it easy to build CNNs for image classification. The torchvision library provides convenient data loading and preprocessing tools."
- **Building an RNN for Sequence Prediction:**
  - We'll create an LSTM for a simple sequence prediction task.
  - **Practical Implementation:**
- Python
- import torch
- import torch.nn as nn
- import numpy as np
-
- # Sample sequence data
- input_size = 3
- hidden_size = 50
- output_size = 3
- sequence_length = 3
- batch_size = 2
-

```python
data = torch.tensor([[[0.1, 0.2, 0.3], [0.2, 0.3, 0.4], [0.3, 0.4, 0.5]],
            [[0.4, 0.5, 0.6], [0.5, 0.6, 0.7], [0.6, 0.7, 0.8]]],
dtype=torch.float32)
labels = torch.tensor([[0.4, 0.5, 0.6], [0.7, 0.8, 0.9]], dtype=torch.float32)

# Define the LSTM architecture
class RNN(nn.Module):
    def __init__(self, input_size, hidden_size, output_size):
        super(RNN, self).__init__()
        self.lstm = nn.LSTM(input_size, hidden_size)
        self.fc = nn.Linear(hidden_size, output_size)

    def forward(self, x):
        out, _ = self.lstm(x.permute(1, 0, 2))
        out = self.fc(out[-1, :, :])
        return out

rnn = RNN(input_size, hidden_size, output_size)
criterion = nn.MSELoss()
optimizer = torch.optim.Adam(rnn.parameters(), lr=0.01)

# Train the RNN
for epoch in range(200):
    outputs = rnn(data)
    loss = criterion(outputs, labels)
    optimizer.zero_grad()
    loss.backward()
```

- optimizer.step()

-

- print("Finished Training")

-

- # Make predictions
- predictions = rnn(data)
- print(predictions)

-

  - **Personal Insight:** "PyTorch's nn.LSTM and nn.RNN layers make it easy to build RNNs for sequence modeling. The dynamic computation graph allows for flexible input sequence lengths."

Key Considerations:

- **Data Loading and Preprocessing:** Use torchvision and torch.utils.data for efficient data handling.
- **Model Architecture:** Choose appropriate layers and architectures for CNNs and RNNs.
- **Loss Function and Optimizer:** Select suitable loss functions and optimizers for your tasks.
- **Training and Evaluation:** Implement proper training and evaluation loops.
- **GPU Acceleration:** Leverage GPU acceleration for faster training..

6.4: TensorFlow vs. PyTorch: A Practical Comparison

We're now going to compare two of the most popular deep learning frameworks: TensorFlow and PyTorch. This section will guide you through their key differences, similarities, and practical considerations.

TensorFlow vs. PyTorch: The Clash of Titans

Both TensorFlow and PyTorch are powerful frameworks, but they have different philosophies and strengths. Let's break down their key aspects.

- **Key Differences:**
  - **Dynamic vs. Static Graphs:**
    - **PyTorch:** Uses a dynamic computation graph, meaning the graph is built on-the-fly during execution. This allows for more flexible and intuitive debugging.
    - **TensorFlow:** Originally used a static computation graph, where the graph is defined before execution. TensorFlow 2.0 introduced eager execution, which provides a dynamic graph option, but it still maintains the option of static graphs through tf.function for performance optimization.
  - **Ease of Use and Debugging:**
    - **PyTorch:** Generally considered more intuitive and easier to debug, especially for research and rapid prototyping.
    - **TensorFlow:** Historically had a steeper learning curve, but TensorFlow 2.0 significantly improved its usability.
  - **Production and Deployment:**
    - **TensorFlow:** Has strong production and deployment capabilities, with TensorFlow Serving and TensorFlow Lite.
    - **PyTorch:** Has been catching up in production deployment with TorchServe and ONNX export.
  -

- Community and Ecosystem:
  - Both have large and active communities.
  - TensorFlow has a more mature ecosystem for production deployment.
  - PyTorch has a strong research community.
- **Practical Comparison: Building a Simple Neural Network**
  - We'll build a simple neural network for a binary classification problem using both frameworks.
  -
  - **PyTorch Implementation:**
- Python

```python
import torch

import torch.nn as nn

import torch.optim as optim

import numpy as np


# Sample data

X = torch.tensor([[1, 2], [2, 3], [3, 4], [8, 9], [9, 10], [10, 11]], dtype=torch.float32)

y = torch.tensor([[0], [0], [0], [1], [1], [1]], dtype=torch.float32)


# Define the model
```

```python
model = nn.Sequential(nn.Linear(2, 1), nn.Sigmoid())


# Define loss and optimizer

criterion = nn.BCELoss()

optimizer = optim.Adam(model.parameters(), lr=0.01)


# Train the model

for epoch in range(100):

    optimizer.zero_grad()

    outputs = model(X)

    loss = criterion(outputs, y)

    loss.backward()

    optimizer.step()


print("PyTorch Training Finished")
```

- o **TensorFlow Implementation:**
  - Python

```python
import tensorflow as tf
```

```python
import numpy as np

# Sample data

X = np.array([[1, 2], [2, 3], [3, 4], [8, 9], [9, 10], [10, 11]], dtype=np.float32)

y = np.array([[0], [0], [0], [1], [1], [1]], dtype=np.float32)


# Define the model

model = tf.keras.Sequential([tf.keras.layers.Dense(1, activation='sigmoid')])


# Define loss and optimizer

model.compile(optimizer='adam', loss='binary_crossentropy')


# Train the model

model.fit(X, y, epochs=100, verbose=0)


print("TensorFlow Training Finished")
```

- o **Personal Insight:** "Both frameworks are capable of building and training neural networks. PyTorch's dynamic graph makes it more intuitive for debugging, while TensorFlow's strong production capabilities make it suitable for large-scale deployments."

- **Practical Considerations:**
  - **Research vs. Production:**
    - PyTorch is often preferred for research due to its flexibility and ease of use.
    - TensorFlow is often preferred for production due to its strong deployment tools.
  - **Community and Support:**
    - Both have large and active communities, providing ample support and resources.
  - **Ecosystem and Tools:**
    - TensorFlow has a more mature ecosystem for production deployment, while PyTorch has a strong and growing ecosystem.
- **Choosing the Right Framework:**
  - The choice between TensorFlow and PyTorch depends on your specific needs and preferences.
  - If you prioritize flexibility and ease of debugging, PyTorch might be a better choice.
  - If you prioritize production deployment and a mature ecosystem, TensorFlow might be a better choice.

Key Considerations:

- **Dynamic vs. Static Graphs:** Understand the differences between dynamic and static graphs.

- **Ease of Use:** Consider your comfort level with each framework's API.

- **Production Capabilities:** Evaluate your deployment needs.

- **Community and Support:** Assess the availability of resources and support.

Chapter 7: Generative AI and Large Language Models (LLMs)

We've covered a lot of ground, but now we're stepping into one of the most exciting areas of AI: generative models and Large Language Models (LLMs). Think of this as giving our machines the ability to create, imagine, and communicate like never before. This chapter will introduce you to the magic behind Transformers, LLMs, GANs, and VAEs. Let's dive into the world of AI creativity.

7.1: Introduction to Transformers and LLM Architecture

We're now venturing into the fascinating world of Transformers and Large Language Models (LLMs), the architectures that have revolutionized natural language processing. This section will guide you through the fundamental concepts and architecture of these powerful models.

Transformers and LLMs: The Language Revolution

Transformers have become the dominant architecture in NLP, surpassing recurrent neural networks (RNNs) in many tasks.LLMs, built upon the Transformer architecture, have demonstrated remarkable capabilities in language generation, understanding, and more. Let's delve into their core components.

- **The Transformer Architecture:**
  - **Attention Mechanism:**
    - The key innovation of Transformers is the attention mechanism, which allows the model to weigh the importance of different words in a sequence when processing it.

- Specifically, the "self-attention" mechanism allows the model to relate different positions of a single sequence in order to compute a representation of the sequence.

- **Multi-Head Attention:**

  - Transformers use multiple attention mechanisms in parallel, called "multi-head attention," to capture different aspects of the input sequence.

- **Encoder-Decoder Structure:**

  - The original Transformer architecture consists of an encoder and a decoder.

  - The encoder processes the input sequence, and the decoder generates the output sequence.

  - Modern LLMs utilize decoder only architectures.

- **Positional Encoding:**

  - Since Transformers do not inherently capture the order of words in a sequence, positional encoding is used to provide information about the position of each word.

  - **Practical Implementation (Simplified Self-Attention):**

- Python

```python
import torch

import torch.nn.functional as F


def self_attention(query, key, value):
```

```python
# query, key, value shape: (batch_size, seq_len, d_k)

d_k = query.size(-1)

scores = torch.matmul(query, key.transpose(-2, -1)) / torch.sqrt(torch.tensor(d_k, dtype=torch.float32))

attention_weights = F.softmax(scores, dim=-1)

output = torch.matmul(attention_weights, value)

return output, attention_weights


# Sample input

batch_size = 2

seq_len = 5

d_k = 64

query = torch.randn(batch_size, seq_len, d_k)

key = torch.randn(batch_size, seq_len, d_k)

value = torch.randn(batch_size, seq_len, d_k)


# Apply self-attention

output, attention_weights = self_attention(query, key, value)
```

```
print("Output Shape:", output.shape)

print("Attention Weights Shape:", attention_weights.shape)
```

-
  - **Expert Commentary:** "The attention mechanism is the core of Transformers, enabling them to capture long-range dependencies in sequences. Multi-head attention allows the model to attend to different aspects of the input simultaneously."
- **Large Language Models (LLMs):**
  - **Decoder-Only Architecture:**
    - Many modern LLMs, such as GPT models, use a decoder-only Transformer architecture.
    - This architecture is well-suited for language generation tasks.
  - **Scaling Up:**
    - LLMs are characterized by their massive size, with billions or even trillions of parameters.
    - Scaling up the size of LLMs has been shown to improve their performance significantly.
  - **Pre-training and Fine-tuning:**
    - LLMs are typically pre-trained on massive amounts of text data using self-supervised learning.
    - They are then fine-tuned on specific tasks using labeled data.
  - **Context Windows:**
    - LLMs have a context window, which is the amount of text the model can consider when generating output. Increasing this context window is an ongoing area of research.
  - **Practical Considerations:**

- LLMs require significant computational resources for training and inference.
- They can exhibit biases and generate toxic language, which are important ethical considerations.

- **Key Components of LLMs:**
  - **Embedding Layer:** Converts input tokens into dense vectors.
  - **Transformer Decoder Layers:** Stacked layers of self-attention and feedforward networks.
  - **Output Layer:** Generates probability distributions over the vocabulary.
- **Personal Insight:** "LLMs have demonstrated remarkable capabilities in language generation and understanding, but they also raise important ethical considerations. It's crucial to address biases and develop responsible AI practices."

Key Considerations:

- **Attention Mechanism:** Understand the self-attention mechanism and its role in capturing dependencies.
- **Transformer Architecture:** Familiarize yourself with the encoder-decoder structure and its variants.
- **LLM Scaling:** Appreciate the impact of scaling up LLM size.
- **Pre-training and Fine-tuning:** Understand the process of pre-training and fine-tuning LLMs.
- **Ethical Considerations:** Be aware of the biases and potential harms of LLMs.

7.2: Working with Pre-trained LLMs via Python APIs

We're now going to dive into the practical side of Large Language Models (LLMs) by interacting with pre-trained models through Python APIs. This section will guide you through accessing and using these powerful models for various NLP tasks.

LLMs at Your Fingertips: Python APIs and Pre-trained Models

Python APIs provide a convenient way to access pre-trained LLMs without needing to train them from scratch. Let's explore how to use these APIs for different applications.

- **Accessing Pre-trained LLMs:**
    - Several providers offer APIs for accessing pre-trained LLMs, including OpenAI, Google Cloud, and Hugging Face.
    - These APIs typically require an API key for authentication.
    - We will focus on the OpenAI API, as it is very common.
    - **Practical Implementation (Using OpenAI API):**
- Python
    - import openai
    - import os
    -
    - # Set your OpenAI API key
    - openai.api_key = os.getenv("OPENAI_API_KEY") # Or set directly as a string
    -
    - def generate_text(prompt):
    - try:

```
response = openai.Completion.create(
    engine="text-davinci-003",  # Or another suitable engine
    prompt=prompt,
    max_tokens=150,
    n=1,
    stop=None,
    temperature=0.7,
)
    return response.choices[0].text.strip()
except Exception as e:
    return f"An error occurred: {e}"

# Example usage
prompt = "Write a short story about a robot who learns to love."
generated_text = generate_text(prompt)
print(generated_text)
```

-

  - **Expert Commentary:** "Using pre-trained LLMs through APIs allows you to leverage state-of-the-art language models without the computational cost of training them yourself. Be sure to handle API keys securely and respect rate limits."

- **Text Generation and Completion:**

  - LLMs can be used to generate and complete text based on a given prompt.

  - **Practical Implementation (Text Completion):**

- Python

  - prompt = "The capital of France is"

- ○ completed_text = generate_text(prompt)
- ○ print(f"{prompt} {completed_text}")

●

- **Question Answering:**
  - ○ LLMs can be used to answer questions based on a given context.
  - ○ **Practical Implementation (Simple Question Answering):**
- Python
  - ○ context = "The Eiffel Tower is a wrought-iron lattice tower on the Champ de Mars in Paris, France."
  - ○ question = "Where is the Eiffel Tower located?"
  - ○ prompt = f"Context: {context}\nQuestion: {question}\nAnswer:"
  - ○ answer = generate_text(prompt)
  - ○ print(answer)

- **Text Summarization:**
  - ○ LLMs can be used to summarize long texts into shorter versions.
  - ○ **Practical Implementation (Text Summarization):**
- Python
  - ○ text = """
  - ○ A large language model (LLM) is a language model notable for its huge size,
  - ○ meaning it is built with a deep neural network with many layers (hence deep) and many parameters,
  - ○ often billions of weights. LLMs can perform general language modeling, but also perform new tasks
  - ○ without specific training, a skill known as zero-shot learning.
  - ○ """
  - ○ prompt = f"Summarize the following text:\n{text}\nSummary:"

- o summary = generate_text(prompt)
- o print(summary)
-
- **Translation:**
  - o LLMs can be used to translate text from one language to another.
  - o **Practical Implementation (Simple Translation):**
- Python
  - o text = "Hello, how are you?"
  - o prompt = f"Translate the following text to French: {text}\nTranslation:"
  - o translation = generate_text(prompt)
  - o print(translation)
- **Key Considerations:**
  - o **API Limits and Costs:** Be aware of API rate limits and costs.
  - o **Prompt Engineering:** Craft effective prompts to get the desired results.
  - o **Model Selection:** Choose the appropriate LLM for your task.
  - o **Data Privacy:** Be mindful of data privacy when using LLM APIs.
  - o **Bias and Ethical Considerations:** Be aware of potential biases in LLM outputs.
- **Personal Insight:** "Prompt engineering is a crucial skill when working with LLMs. By crafting clear and specific prompts, you can guide the model to generate the desired outputs. It is also important to be aware of the models limiations."

7.3: Fine-tuning LLMs for Specific Tasks

We're now going to explore the powerful technique of fine-tuning Large Language Models (LLMs) to make them perform even better on specific tasks. This section will guide you through the process, considerations, and practical aspects of fine-tuning.

Fine-tuning LLMs: Tailoring Power for Precision

Fine-tuning allows you to take a pre-trained LLM and adapt it to your specific needs by training it on a smaller, task-specific dataset. This can significantly improve performance compared to zero-shot or few-shot learning.

- **Understanding Fine-tuning:**
  - **Transfer Learning:** Fine-tuning is a form of transfer learning, where knowledge gained from pre-training is transferred to a new task.
  - **Task-Specific Data:** You'll need a dataset that is relevant to the task you want to fine-tune the LLM for.
  - **Computational Cost:** Fine-tuning requires less computational resources than pre-training, but it still requires significant GPU power.
  - **Practical Considerations:**
    - The quality and size of your fine-tuning dataset are crucial.
    - Overfitting can occur if the dataset is too small or if the model is fine-tuned for too long.
- **Fine-tuning Process:**
  - **Prepare the Dataset:** Format your data into a suitable format for the LLM.
  - **Load the Pre-trained Model:** Load the pre-trained LLM you want to fine-tune.

- o **Define the Training Parameters:** Set the learning rate, batch size, and number of epochs.
- o **Train the Model:** Train the LLM on your task-specific dataset.
- o **Evaluate the Model:** Evaluate the performance of the fine-tuned model on a validation set.
- o **Practical Implementation (Conceptual Example with Hugging Face Transformers):**

- Python
- from transformers import AutoTokenizer, AutoModelForCausalLM, TrainingArguments, Trainer
- from datasets import Dataset
-
- # Sample dataset (replace with your actual data)
- data = [
-     {"text": "Translate to French: Hello, world!", "label": "Bonjour, monde!"},
-     {"text": "Translate to French: How are you?", "label": "Comment allez-vous?"},
-     # ... more data
-]
-
- dataset = Dataset.from_list(data)
-
- # Load tokenizer and model
- tokenizer = AutoTokenizer.from_pretrained("gpt2") # Example model. Use a model that fits your needs.
- model = AutoModelForCausalLM.from_pretrained("gpt2")

```
# Tokenize the dataset
def tokenize_function(examples):
    return tokenizer(examples["text"], padding="max_length", truncation=True)

tokenized_datasets = dataset.map(tokenize_function, batched=True)

# Define training arguments
training_args = TrainingArguments(
    output_dir="./results",
    num_train_epochs=3,
    per_device_train_batch_size=8,
    logging_dir="./logs",
)

# Define trainer
trainer = Trainer(
    model=model,
    args=training_args,
    train_dataset=tokenized_datasets,
)

# Train the model
trainer.train()

# Example of how to use the fine tuned model.
```

- input_text = "Translate to French: Where is the library?"
- input_ids = tokenizer.encode(input_text, return_tensors="pt")
- output = model.generate(input_ids, max_length=50, num_return_sequences=1)
- print(tokenizer.decode(output[0], skip_special_tokens=True))
-
  - **Expert Commentary:** "Fine-tuning allows you to specialize a powerful LLM for your specific needs. The quality of the fine-tuning dataset is critical for achieving good performance."
- **Key Considerations:**
  - **Dataset Size and Quality:** A larger and higher-quality dataset will generally lead to better performance.
  - **Learning Rate and Epochs:** Tune these hyperparameters to avoid overfitting or underfitting.
  - **Model Selection:** Choose a pre-trained LLM that is suitable for your task.
  - **Evaluation Metrics:** Use appropriate evaluation metrics to assess the performance of the fine-tuned model.
  - **Computational Resources:** Fine-tuning can be computationally expensive, especially for large LLMs.
- **Practical Applications:**
  - **Text Classification:** Fine-tune an LLM to classify text into specific categories.
  - **Question Answering:** Fine-tune an LLM to answer questions based on a specific knowledge base.
  - **Text Summarization:** Fine-tune an LLM to generate summaries of specific types of documents.

- **Code Generation:** Fine-tune an LLM to generate code in a specific programming language.
- **Chatbot Development:** Fine tune an LLM to provide more relevant and specific responses for a chatbot.

- **Personal Insight:** "Fine-tuning LLMs is a powerful technique for adapting these models to specific tasks. It allows you to leverage the general knowledge of a pre-trained LLM and tailor it to your particular needs.

7.4: Generative Adversarial Networks (GANs) and Variational Autoencoders (VAEs)

We're now diving into the world of Generative Adversarial Networks (GANs) and Variational Autoencoders (VAEs), two powerful techniques for generating new data. This section will guide you through their architectures, training processes, and practical applications.

GANs and VAEs: The Creators of New Data

GANs and VAEs are both used to generate new data, but they approach the problem in different ways. GANs use a competitive training process, while VAEs use a probabilistic approach.

- **Generative Adversarial Networks (GANs): The Adversarial Duo**
  - **Architecture:** GANs consist of two neural networks: a generator and a discriminator.
    - **Generator:** Creates fake data samples.
    - **Discriminator:** Distinguishes between real and fake data samples.

- ○ **Training Process:** The generator and discriminator are trained in an adversarial manner. The generator tries to fool the discriminator, while the discriminator tries to correctly identify fake samples. This competitive process drives both networks to improve.

  - ○

  - ○ **Practical Implementation (Simple GAN for MNIST):**

- • Python

```python
import torch

import torch.nn as nn

import torch.optim as optim

from torchvision import datasets, transforms

from torch.utils.data import DataLoader


# Define the generator

class Generator(nn.Module):

    def __init__(self, latent_dim, img_shape):

        super(Generator, self).__init__()

        self.model = nn.Sequential(

            nn.Linear(latent_dim, 128),
```

```python
            nn.ReLU(),

            nn.Linear(128, 256),

            nn.ReLU(),

            nn.Linear(256, 784),

            nn.Tanh()

        )

        self.img_shape = img_shape


    def forward(self, z):

        img = self.model(z)

        img = img.view(img.size(0), *self.img_shape)

        return img


# Define the discriminator

class Discriminator(nn.Module):

    def __init__(self, img_shape):

        super(Discriminator, self).__init__()

        self.model = nn.Sequential(
```

```python
            nn.Linear(784, 256),

            nn.ReLU(),

            nn.Linear(256, 128),

            nn.ReLU(),

            nn.Linear(128, 1),

            nn.Sigmoid()

        )


    def forward(self, img):

        img_flat = img.view(img.size(0), -1)

        validity = self.model(img_flat)

        return validity


# Load MNIST dataset

transform = transforms.Compose([transforms.ToTensor(),
transforms.Normalize((0.5,), (0.5,))])

dataloader = DataLoader(datasets.MNIST('./data', train=True, download=True,
transform=transform), batch_size=64, shuffle=True)
```

```python
# Initialize generator and discriminator

latent_dim = 100

img_shape = (1, 28, 28)

generator = Generator(latent_dim, img_shape)

discriminator = Discriminator(img_shape)


# Define loss function and optimizers

adversarial_loss = nn.BCELoss()

optimizer_G = optim.Adam(generator.parameters(), lr=0.0002, betas=(0.5, 0.999))

optimizer_D = optim.Adam(discriminator.parameters(), lr=0.0002, betas=(0.5, 0.999))


# Training loop (simplified)
for epoch in range(5):
    for i, (imgs, _) in enumerate(dataloader):
        # Train discriminator

        real_validity = discriminator(imgs)

        fake_imgs = generator(torch.randn(imgs.size(0), latent_dim))
```

```python
fake_validity = discriminator(fake_imgs.detach())

d_loss = (adversarial_loss(real_validity, torch.ones_like(real_validity)) +
adversarial_loss(fake_validity, torch.zeros_like(fake_validity))) / 2

optimizer_D.zero_grad()

d_loss.backward()

optimizer_D.step()


# Train generator

fake_imgs = generator(torch.randn(imgs.size(0), latent_dim))

g_loss = adversarial_loss(discriminator(fake_imgs),
torch.ones_like(real_validity))

optimizer_G.zero_grad()

g_loss.backward()

optimizer_G.step()
```

-
  - **Expert Commentary:** "GANs are powerful for generating realistic data, but they can be challenging to train due to instability. The adversarial training process requires careful tuning of hyperparameters."
- **Variational Autoencoders (VAEs): The Probabilistic Generators**
  - **Architecture:** VAEs consist of an encoder and a decoder.

- **Encoder:** Encodes the input data into a latent space distribution.
- **Decoder:** Decodes samples from the latent space distribution into generated data.
  - **Training Process:** VAEs are trained to minimize the reconstruction error and the Kullback-Leibler (KL) divergence between the latent space distribution and a prior distribution.
  - **Practical Considerations:** VAEs tend to generate smoother and less sharp images compared to GANs.
  - **Concise Explanation:** VAEs learn a probabilistic mapping from input data to a latent space, which allows for controlled generation of new samples.

- **Key Considerations:**
  - **Stability:** GANs can be unstable during training.
  - **Mode Collapse:** GANs can suffer from mode collapse, where the generator produces limited variations of output.
  - **Latent Space:** VAEs provide a structured latent space that can be used for interpolation and manipulation.

- **Practical Applications:**
  - **Image Generation:** Generating realistic images.
  - **Image-to-Image Translation:** Translating images from one domain to another.
  - **Text Generation:** Generating realistic text.
  - **Anomaly Detection:** Identifying anomalies in data.

- **Personal Insight:** "GANs and VAEs are both powerful tools for generating new data, but they have different strengths and weaknesses. GANs excel at generating realistic images, while VAEs provide a structured latent space that can be used for controlled generation."

Chapter 8: Natural Language Processing (NLP) Applications

We've journeyed through various AI domains, and now it's time to focus on the fascinating world of Natural Language Processing (NLP). Think of NLP as giving machines the ability to understand, interpret, and generate human language. In this chapter, we'll dive into practical NLP applications, from text preprocessing to building chatbots. Let's make machines talk!

8.1: Text Preprocessing and Analysis with NLTK and spaCy

We're now diving into the world of Natural Language Processing (NLP) with two powerful libraries: NLTK and spaCy. This section will guide you through the essential steps of text preprocessing and analysis.

NLTK and spaCy: Your NLP Toolbelt

NLTK (Natural Language Toolkit) and spaCy are popular Python libraries for NLP. NLTK is known for its comprehensive set of tools and educational resources, while spaCy is known for its speed and efficiency in production environments.

- **Text Preprocessing: Cleaning and Preparing Your Data**
  - **Tokenization:** Breaking text into individual words or subwords.
    - **NLTK Implementation:**
  - Python

```
import nltk

from nltk.tokenize import word_tokenize
```

```
nltk.download('punkt') # Download necessary resources
```

```
text = "Hello, world! This is a sample sentence."
```

```
tokens = word_tokenize(text)
```

```
print("NLTK Tokens:", tokens)
```

- **spaCy Implementation:**
  - Python

```
import spacy
```

```
nlp = spacy.load("en_core_web_sm") # Load a small English model
```

```
doc = nlp(text)
```

```
tokens = [token.text for token in doc]
```

```
print("spaCy Tokens:", tokens)
```

- **Lowercasing:** Converting text to lowercase.
  - **Practical Implementation:**
    - Python

```
lowercase_tokens = [token.lower() for token in tokens]
```

```
print("Lowercase Tokens:", lowercase_tokens)
```

- ○ **Removing Punctuation:** Removing punctuation marks.
  - ■ **Practical Implementation:**
- ○ Python

```
import string
```

```
no_punct_tokens = [token for token in lowercase_tokens if token not in
string.punctuation]
```

```
print("No Punctuation Tokens:", no_punct_tokens)
```

- ○
- ○
- ○ **Removing Stop Words:** Removing common words like "a," "an," and "the."
  - ■ **NLTK Implementation:**
- ○ Python

```
from nltk.corpus import stopwords
```

```python
nltk.download('stopwords')

stop_words = set(stopwords.words('english'))

filtered_tokens = [token for token in no_punct_tokens if token not in stop_words]

print("Filtered Tokens (NLTK):", filtered_tokens)
```

- o
    - ■ **spaCy Implementation:**
  - o Python

```python
filtered_tokens = [token.text for token in doc if not token.is_stop and not token.is_punct]

print("Filtered Tokens (spaCy):", filtered_tokens)
```

- o **Stemming and Lemmatization:** Reducing words to their root form.[3]
    - ■ **NLTK Stemming:**
  - o Python

```python
from nltk.stem import PorterStemmer

stemmer = PorterStemmer()

stemmed_tokens = [stemmer.stem(token) for token in filtered_tokens]
```

```
print("Stemmed Tokens:", stemmed_tokens)
```

    ○

       ■ **spaCy Lemmatization:**

    ○ Python

```
lemmatized_tokens = [token.lemma_ for token in doc if not token.is_stop and not token.is_punct]

print("Lemmatized Tokens:", lemmatized_tokens)
```

    ○ **Expert Commentary:** "Text preprocessing is crucial for NLP tasks. It cleans and prepares the text data, making it easier for models to understand and process. spaCy's processing pipeline and linguistic annotations make it efficient for real-world applications."

- **Text Analysis: Extracting Meaning and Insights**
  - **Part-of-Speech (POS) Tagging:** Assigning grammatical tags to words.
    - **NLTK Implementation:**
  - Python

```
nltk.download('averaged_perceptron_tagger')

pos_tags = nltk.pos_tag(tokens)

print("POS Tags (NLTK):", pos_tags)
```

    ○

- **spaCy Implementation:**
  - Python

```python
pos_tags = [(token.text, token.pos_) for token in doc]

print("POS Tags (spaCy):", pos_tags)
```

  -
  -
  - **Named Entity Recognition (NER):** Identifying named entities like people, locations, and organizations.
    - **spaCy Implementation:**
      - Python

```python
entities = [(ent.text, ent.label_) for ent in doc.ents]

print("Named Entities:", entities)
```

  - **Dependency Parsing:** Analyzing the grammatical structure of sentences.
    - **spaCy Implementation:**
      - Python

```python
dependencies = [(token.text, token.dep_, token.head.text) for token in doc]

print("Dependencies:", dependencies)
```

- **Sentiment Analysis:** Determining the sentiment or emotion expressed in text.
  - **NLTK Implementation (using VADER):**
    - Python

```python
from nltk.sentiment import SentimentIntensityAnalyzer


nltk.download('vader_lexicon')

analyzer = SentimentIntensityAnalyzer()

sentiment = analyzer.polarity_scores(text)

print("Sentiment (NLTK VADER):", sentiment)
```

  -
  - **spaCy Implementation (using TextBlob):**
    - Python

```python
from textblob import TextBlob


blob = TextBlob(text)

sentiment = blob.sentiment

print("Sentiment (spaCy TextBlob):", sentiment)
```

- **Personal Insight:** "spaCy's efficient processing pipeline and pre-trained models make it a powerful tool for real-world NLP applications. NLTK's extensive resources and educational focus make it a great choice for learning and experimenting with NLP."

- **Key Considerations:**
  - **Language Models:** Choose appropriate language models for your tasks.
  - **Preprocessing Pipeline:** Design a preprocessing pipeline that fits your data and objectives.
  - **Performance:** Consider the performance trade-offs between NLTK and spaCy.
  - **Data Quality:** NLP models are sensitive to data quality.

8.2: Sentiment Analysis, Text Classification, Summarization

We're now diving into three core NLP tasks: sentiment analysis, text classification, and summarization. This section will guide you through the concepts, implementations, and practical applications of these essential techniques.

NLP in Action: Extracting Insights and Meaning

These three tasks are fundamental in extracting meaningful information from text data. Let's explore how they work.

- **Sentiment Analysis: Understanding Emotions in Text**
  - **Concept:** Determining the emotional tone or sentiment expressed in a piece of text (e.g., positive, negative, neutral).
  - **Practical Implementation (Using TextBlob):**
- Python

```
from textblob import TextBlob

def analyze_sentiment(text):
    blob = TextBlob(text)
    sentiment = blob.sentiment.polarity  # Polarity: -1 (negative) to 1 (positive)
    if sentiment > 0:
        return "Positive"
    elif sentiment < 0:
        return "Negative"
    else:
        return "Neutral"

text = "This movie was absolutely fantastic!"
sentiment = analyze_sentiment(text)
print(f"Sentiment: {sentiment}")

text2 = "This product is terrible, I hate it."
sentiment2 = analyze_sentiment(text2)
print(f"Sentiment: {sentiment2}")
```

-
  - **Expert Commentary:** "Sentiment analysis is powerful for understanding customer feedback, social media trends, and more. TextBlob offers a simple and effective way to get sentiment scores, although more advanced models can offer better accuracy."
- **Text Classification: Categorizing Text Data**
  - **Concept:** Assigning predefined categories or labels to text documents.

- o **Practical Implementation (Using Scikit-learn and TF-IDF):**
- Python
  - o from sklearn.model_selection import train_test_split
  - o from sklearn.feature_extraction.text import TfidfVectorizer
  - o from sklearn.naive_bayes import MultinomialNB
  - o from sklearn.metrics import classification_report
  - o
  - o # Sample dataset
  - o data = [
  - o ("This is a sports article.", "sports"),
  - o ("The stock market is down today.", "finance"),
  - o ("A new movie was released.", "entertainment"),
  - o ("The game was very exciting", "sports"),
  - o ("Company profit increased", "finance"),
  - o ("The new album sold very well", "entertainment")
  - o]
  - o
  - o texts = [item[0] for item in data]
  - o labels = [item[1] for item in data]
  - o
  - o # Split data
  - o X_train, X_test, y_train, y_test = train_test_split(texts, labels, test_size=0.2, random_state=42)
  - o
  - o # Vectorize text using TF-IDF
  - o vectorizer = TfidfVectorizer()
  - o X_train_vectors = vectorizer.fit_transform(X_train)

- X_test_vectors = vectorizer.transform(X_test)
-
- # Train a Naive Bayes classifier
- classifier = MultinomialNB()
- classifier.fit(X_train_vectors, y_train)
-
- # Make predictions
- predictions = classifier.predict(X_test_vectors)
-
- # Evaluate the model
- print(classification_report(y_test, predictions))

-

  - **Personal Insight:** "Text classification is a versatile technique used in various applications, from spam detection to topic categorization. TF-IDF and Naive Bayes provide a simple yet effective baseline."

- **Text Summarization: Condensing Text Information**
  - **Concept:** Generating a shorter version of a text document that retains its key information.
  - **Practical Implementation (Using Gensim):**
- Python
  - from gensim.summarization import summarize
  -
  - text = """
  - The rapid development of artificial intelligence (AI) has led to significant advancements in various fields.
  - AI algorithms are now capable of performing complex tasks, such as image recognition, natural language processing,

- and decision-making. These advancements have opened up new possibilities for automation and innovation. However,
- the increasing capabilities of AI also raise ethical concerns, including job displacement and data privacy.
- It is crucial to develop guidelines and regulations to ensure the responsible use of AI.
- """
-
- summary = summarize(text, ratio=0.3) # Summarize to 30% of original length
- print(f"Summary:\n{summary}")

-
  - **Concise Explanation:** Gensim provides a convenient way to generate extractive summaries, which select key sentences from the original text. Abstractive summarization, which generates new sentences, is more advanced and often uses deep learning models.

- **Key Considerations:**
  - **Data Quality:** NLP models are sensitive to the quality of the input data.
  - **Preprocessing:** Proper text preprocessing is crucial for accurate results.
  - **Model Selection:** Choose appropriate models based on the task and data.
  - **Evaluation Metrics:** Use appropriate metrics to evaluate model performance.

- **Practical Applications:**
  - **Sentiment Analysis:** Customer feedback analysis, social media monitoring.
  - **Text Classification:** Spam detection, topic categorization, news classification.
  - **Text Summarization:** News summarization, document summarization, report summarization.

8.3: Building Practical Chatbots and NLP Applications

We're now going to put our knowledge into action by building practical chatbots and other NLP applications. This section will guide you through the concepts, implementations, and real-world considerations.

NLP in Practice: Conversational AI and More

Let's explore how to create chatbots and other applications that leverage the power of NLP.

- **Building a Simple Rule-Based Chatbot:**
  - **Concept:** Chatbots that respond based on predefined rules and patterns.
  - **Practical Implementation:**
- Python

```
def simple_chatbot(user_input):
```

```python
    user_input = user_input.lower()

    if "hello" in user_input or "hi" in user_input:

        return "Hello! How can I help you?"

    elif "how are you" in user_input:

        return "I'm doing well, thank you!"

    elif "what is the weather" in user_input:

        return "I'm sorry, I cannot provide real-time weather information."

    elif "goodbye" in user_input or "bye" in user_input:

        return "Goodbye! Have a nice day."

    else:

        return "I don't understand. Can you please rephrase?"


# Example interaction

while True:

    user_input = input("You: ")

    if user_input.lower() == "exit":

        break
```

```
response = simple_chatbot(user_input)

print("Chatbot:", response)
```

-

  - **Expert Commentary:** "Rule-based chatbots are simple to implement and effective for basic interactions. However, they lack the flexibility and understanding of more advanced models."
- **Building a Chatbot with Intent Recognition:**
  - **Concept:** Chatbots that use machine learning to understand user intents and provide relevant responses.
  - **Practical Implementation (Using Scikit-learn and TF-IDF):**
- Python

```
from sklearn.model_selection import train_test_split

from sklearn.feature_extraction.text import TfidfVectorizer

from sklearn.naive_bayes import MultinomialNB

# Sample dataset (intents and responses)

data = [

    ("Hello", "greeting"),

    ("Hi", "greeting"),

    ("How are you", "greeting"),
```

```python
    ("What is the weather", "weather"),

    ("Tell me the forecast", "weather"),

    ("Goodbye", "goodbye"),

    ("Bye", "goodbye"),

]


texts = [item[0] for item in data]

labels = [item[1] for item in data]


# Vectorize text using TF-IDF

vectorizer = TfidfVectorizer()

X_vectors = vectorizer.fit_transform(texts)


# Train a Naive Bayes classifier

classifier = MultinomialNB()

classifier.fit(X_vectors, labels)


def intent_chatbot(user_input):
```

```python
    user_vector = vectorizer.transform([user_input])

    intent = classifier.predict(user_vector)[0]


    if intent == "greeting":

        return "Hello! How can I help you?"

    elif intent == "weather":

        return "I'm sorry, I cannot provide real-time weather information."

    elif intent == "goodbye":

        return "Goodbye! Have a nice day."

    else:

        return "I don't understand. Can you please rephrase?"


# Example interaction
while True:

    user_input = input("You: ")

    if user_input.lower() == "exit":

        break

    response = intent_chatbot(user_input)
```

```
print("Chatbot:", response)
```

-
  - **Personal Insight:** "Intent recognition allows chatbots to understand the user's purpose, leading to more relevant and helpful responses. This approach can be expanded with more sophisticated models and larger datasets."

- **Other Practical NLP Applications:**
  - **Text Summarization for News Articles:** Automatically generate summaries of news articles.
  - **Sentiment Analysis for Social Media Monitoring:** Analyze social media posts to understand public sentiment.
  - **Named Entity Recognition for Information Extraction:** Extract key information from unstructured text.
  - **Machine Translation for Multilingual Support:** Translate text from one language to another.
  - **Question Answering Systems:** Build systems that can answer questions based on a given context.

- **Key Considerations:**
  - **Data Quality:** NLP models are sensitive to data quality.
  - **Preprocessing:** Proper text preprocessing is crucial.
  - **Model Selection:** Choose appropriate models based on the task and data.
  - **Evaluation:** Evaluate model performance using appropriate metrics.
  - **User Experience:** Design chatbots with a focus on user experience.
  - **Ethical Considerations:** Be mindful of biases and ethical implications.

-

- **Practical Applications:**

  - **Customer Support Chatbots:** Provide automated support and answer customer queries.[6]

  - **Information Retrieval Systems:** Build systems that can retrieve relevant information from large text datasets.

  - **Content Moderation Tools:** Automatically identify and filter inappropriate content.

  - **Voice Assistants:** Develop voice-based interfaces for various applications.

Chapter 9: Reinforcement Learning in Practice

We've explored supervised and unsupervised learning, and now it's time to delve into the exciting realm of reinforcement learning (RL). Think of RL as teaching machines to learn through trial and error, like training a puppy with rewards. In this chapter, we'll cover Q-learning, deep RL, and practical applications in games and robotics. Let's start rewarding our machines!.

9.1: Q-Learning and Deep Reinforcement Learning

We're now venturing into the exciting world of reinforcement learning (RL), where agents learn to make decisions by interacting with an environment. This section will guide you through Q-learning and Deep Reinforcement Learning (DRL), two fundamental techniques in RL.

Reinforcement Learning: Learning Through Interaction

RL is about training agents to maximize cumulative rewards in an environment. Let's explore how Q-learning and DRL achieve this.

- **Q-Learning: Learning Optimal Actions**
  - **Concept:** Q-learning is a model-free RL algorithm that learns an optimal policy by estimating the Q-values, which represent the expected cumulative reward for taking an action in a given state.
  - **Q-Table:** Q-learning typically uses a Q-table to store Q-values for each state-action pair.
  - **Update Rule:** The Q-table is updated using the Bellman equation, which iteratively refines the Q-values based on observed rewards and future Q-values.
  - **Practical Implementation (Simple Q-Learning Example):**

- Python

```python
import numpy as np

# Define environment (simple grid world)
states = [0, 1, 2, 3, 4, 5]
actions = [0, 1]  # 0: left, 1: right
rewards = np.array([0, 0, 0, 0, 10, -1])  # Rewards for each state

# Initialize Q-table
q_table = np.zeros((len(states), len(actions)))

# Q-learning parameters
alpha = 0.1  # Learning rate
gamma = 0.9  # Discount factor
epsilon = 0.1  # Exploration rate
episodes = 1000
```

```python
# Q-learning algorithm

for episode in range(episodes):

    state = 0  # Start at state 0

    done = False


    while not done:

        # Choose action (epsilon-greedy policy)

        if np.random.rand() < epsilon:

            action = np.random.choice(actions)  # Explore

        else:

            action = np.argmax(q_table[state])  # Exploit


        # Take action and observe next state and reward

        if action == 0:  # Left

            next_state = max(0, state - 1)

        else:  # Right

            next_state = min(len(states) - 1, state + 1)
```

```python
reward = rewards[next_state]

# Update Q-table

q_table[state, action] = q_table[state, action] + alpha * (reward + gamma *
np.max(q_table[next_state]) - q_table[state, action])


state = next_state


if state == 4 or state == 5:  # Terminal states

    done = True


print("Q-table:")

print(q_table)
```

- **Expert Commentary:** "Q-learning is effective for small state-action spaces.[4]However, it becomes impractical for large or continuous spaces due to the size of the Q-table."
- **Deep Reinforcement Learning (DRL): Scaling Up with Neural Networks**
  - **Concept:** DRL combines Q-learning with deep neural networks to approximate the Q-values.
  - **Deep Q-Network (DQN):** DQN uses a neural network to estimate Q-values, allowing it to handle high-dimensional state spaces.

- **Experience Replay:** DQN stores past experiences in a replay buffer and samples mini-batches to train the network, improving stability and data efficiency.
- **Target Network:** DQN uses a separate target network to stabilize training by providing a fixed target for Q-value updates.
- **Practical Considerations:** DRL can be computationally expensive and requires careful tuning of hyperparameters.
- **Concise Explanation:** DRL extends traditional Q-learning by using deep neural networks to approximate the Q-function, enabling agents to learn in complex environments.

- **Key Considerations:**
  - **Exploration-Exploitation Trade-off:** Balance exploration (trying new actions) and exploitation (using known good actions).
  - **Reward Design:** Define a reward function that guides the agent towards the desired behavior.
  - **State Representation:** Choose an appropriate representation of the environment's state.
  - **Hyperparameter Tuning:** Tune hyperparameters like learning rate, discount factor, and exploration rate.
  - **Stability:** DRL training can be unstable, requiring techniques like experience replay and target networks.

- **Practical Applications:**
  - **Game Playing:** Training agents to play video games.
  - **Robotics:** Controlling robots to perform complex tasks.
  - **Autonomous Driving:** Developing self-driving cars.
  - **Resource Management:** Optimizing resource allocation in various domains.

- **Personal Insight:** "DRL has revolutionized RL by enabling agents to learn in complex, high-dimensional environments.[15] However, it's crucial to carefully design the reward function and tune hyperparameters for successful training."

9.2: Practical Applications in Game Playing and Robotics

We're now exploring the real-world impact of reinforcement learning (RL) by focusing on two exciting applications: game playing and robotics. This section will guide you through the concepts, implementations, and challenges of applying RL in these domains.

RL in Action: Mastering Games and Controlling Machines

RL has demonstrated remarkable success in both game playing and robotics, pushing the boundaries of what AI can achieve. Let's delve into these applications.

- **Game Playing: Achieving Superhuman Performance**
  - **Concept:** Training AI agents to play games at or above human-level performance.
  - **Deep Q-Networks (DQNs):** DQNs have been used to achieve impressive results in Atari games and other environments.
  - **AlphaGo and AlphaZero:** DeepMind's AlphaGo and AlphaZero demonstrated the power of RL in complex games like Go and chess.
  - **Practical Implementation (Simple DQN for CartPole):**

```
import gym

import numpy as np
```

```python
import random

import torch

import torch.nn as nn

import torch.optim as optim

# Define DQN architecture

class DQN(nn.Module):

    def __init__(self, state_size, action_size):

        super(DQN, self).__init__()

        self.fc1 = nn.Linear(state_size, 128)

        self.relu = nn.ReLU()

        self.fc2 = nn.Linear(128, action_size)


    def forward(self, x):

        x = self.relu(self.fc1(x))

        x = self.fc2(x)

        return x


# Initialize environment and DQN
```

```python
env = gym.make('CartPole-v1')

state_size = env.observation_space.shape[0]

action_size = env.action_space.n

dqn = DQN(state_size, action_size)

optimizer = optim.Adam(dqn.parameters(), lr=0.001)

loss_fn = nn.MSELoss()


# Experience replay buffer

replay_buffer = []

batch_size = 32


# Training loop (simplified)

episodes = 200

gamma = 0.99


for episode in range(episodes):

    state = env.reset()

    done = False
```

```python
while not done:

    # Choose action (epsilon-greedy)

    if random.random() < 0.1:

        action = env.action_space.sample()

    else:

        state_tensor = torch.FloatTensor(state).unsqueeze(0)

        q_values = dqn(state_tensor)

        action = torch.argmax(q_values).item()


    next_state, reward, done, _ = env.step(action)

    replay_buffer.append((state, action, reward, next_state, done))


    # Train DQN

    if len(replay_buffer) > batch_size:

        batch = random.sample(replay_buffer, batch_size)

        states, actions, rewards, next_states, dones = zip(*batch)
```

```python
states_tensor = torch.FloatTensor(states)

actions_tensor = torch.LongTensor(actions).unsqueeze(1)

rewards_tensor = torch.FloatTensor(rewards)

next_states_tensor = torch.FloatTensor(next_states)

dones_tensor = torch.FloatTensor(dones)


q_values = dqn(states_tensor).gather(1, actions_tensor).squeeze(1)

next_q_values = dqn(next_states_tensor).max(1)[0]

target_q_values = rewards_tensor + (1 - dones_tensor) * gamma * next_q_values


loss = loss_fn(q_values, target_q_values.detach())

optimizer.zero_grad()

loss.backward()

optimizer.step()


state = next_state
```

```
print(f"Episode: {episode + 1}, Score: {env._elapsed_steps}")
```

```
env.close()
```

```
```

* **Expert Commentary:** "RL has revolutionized game playing by enabling AI agents to learn complex strategies and achieve superhuman performance. However, training RL agents for complex games can be computationally expensive."

- **Robotics: Enabling Autonomous Machines**
  - **Concept:** Training robots to perform complex tasks in real-world environments.
  - **Challenges:** Robotics environments are often complex, continuous, and noisy.
  - **Deep Reinforcement Learning (DRL):** DRL algorithms are used to train robots for tasks like grasping, navigation, and manipulation.
  - **Simulation and Sim-to-Real Transfer:** Simulation environments are often used to train robots, and sim-to-real transfer techniques are used to bridge the gap between simulation and real-world environments.
  - **Practical Considerations:**
    - Robot hardware limitations and sensor noise.
    - Safety and robustness in real-world environments.
    - Data efficiency and sample complexity.

- **Key Considerations:**
  - **Reward Design:** Define a reward function that guides the agent towards the desired behavior.
  - **Exploration-Exploitation Trade-off:** Balance exploration and exploitation.
  - **State Representation:** Choose an appropriate representation of the environment's state.
  - **Hyperparameter Tuning:** Tune hyperparameters for optimal performance.
  - **Computational Resources:** Training RL agents can be computationally expensive.
- **Practical Applications:**
  - **Game Playing:** Atari games, Go, chess, video games.
  - **Robotics:** Grasping, navigation, manipulation, autonomous vehicles.
  - **Industrial Automation:** Optimizing manufacturing processes, controlling robots in factories.
  - **Healthcare:** Developing robotic surgical assistants, personalized treatment plans.
- **Personal Insight:** "RL has the potential to revolutionize robotics by enabling autonomous machines to perform complex tasks in real-world environments. However, addressing the challenges of hardware limitations, safety, and data efficiency is crucial for successful deployment."

Your RL Application Arsenal

You've now learned about the practical applications of RL in game playing and robotics. Remember to design effective reward functions, balance exploration and exploitation, and address the challenges of real-world environments. Let's move on to advanced RL techniques.

Chapter 10: AI Deployment and Scalability

We've built some amazing AI models, but they're not much use if they just sit on our laptops. This chapter is all about taking your AI creations and making them available to the world. We'll explore deploying models to cloud platforms, building scalable applications, and using Docker for containerization. Let's get your AI out there!

10.1: Deploying AI Models to Cloud Platforms

We're now stepping into the world of cloud deployment, where we'll learn how to make our AI models accessible to the world. This section will guide you through the process of deploying models to cloud platforms, focusing on key concepts and practical implementations.

Cloud Deployment: Bringing AI to the Masses

Cloud platforms offer scalable and reliable infrastructure for deploying AI models. Let's explore how to make our models available as services.

- **Key Concepts:**
  - **Containerization (Docker):** Packaging your model and its dependencies into a container for consistent deployment across different environments.
  - **Orchestration (Kubernetes):** Managing and scaling containerized applications.
  - **Serverless Functions (AWS Lambda, Google Cloud Functions):** Deploying models as serverless functions for event-driven processing.
  - **Model Serving (TensorFlow Serving, TorchServe):** Optimizing model serving for high-performance inference.

- ○ **API Endpoints:** Exposing your model as an API endpoint for easy integration with other applications.
- **Deployment Process:**
  - ○ **Model Serialization:** Save your trained model in a format suitable for deployment (e.g., SavedModel, ONNX).
  - ○ **Containerization:** Create a Docker container that includes your model, dependencies, and serving logic.
  - ○ **Cloud Deployment:** Deploy the container to a cloud platform (e.g., AWS, Google Cloud, Azure).
  - ○ **API Exposure:** Create an API endpoint to access your model.
  - ○ **Monitoring and Scaling:** Monitor model performance and scale resources as needed.
- **Practical Implementation (Docker and Flask for Simple Model Serving):**
  - ○ We'll demonstrate a basic example using Docker and Flask to serve a simple model.
  - ○ **Model Saving (Conceptual):**
- Python

```
# Sample model (conceptual)

import pickle

from sklearn.linear_model import LinearRegression



model = LinearRegression()
```

```python
# Train the model...

pickle.dump(model, open('model.pkl', 'wb'))
```

-
  - **Flask API:**
- Python

```python
from flask import Flask, request, jsonify

import pickle

import numpy as np


app = Flask(__name__)

model = pickle.load(open('model.pkl', 'rb'))


@app.route('/predict', methods=['POST'])

def predict():

    data = request.get_json()

    input_data = np.array(data['input']).reshape(1, -1)

    prediction = model.predict(input_data).tolist()

    return jsonify({'prediction': prediction})
```

```python
if __name__ == '__main__':

    app.run(debug=True, host='0.0.0.0', port=5000)
```

- ○ **Dockerfile:**
- Dockerfile

```dockerfile
FROM python:3.8-slim

WORKDIR /app

COPY requirements.txt .

RUN pip install -r requirements.txt

COPY . .

EXPOSE 5000

CMD ["python", "app.py"]
```

- ○ **requirements.txt:**

- Plaintext

Flask

scikit-learn

numpy

  - **Building and Running the Docker Container:**
- Bash

```
docker build -t my-model-api .

docker run -p 5000:5000 my-model-api
```

  - **Explanation:** This example builds a simple API for a scikit-learn model. The Dockerfile sets up a Python environment, installs dependencies, copies the application code, and runs the Flask app.
- **Cloud Platform Deployment (Conceptual):**
  - For actual cloud deployment, you would typically use services like AWS ECS, Google Cloud Run, or Azure Container Instances.
  - These services allow you to deploy Docker containers and manage scaling and networking.
- **Key Considerations:**
  - **Scalability:** Design your deployment for scalability to handle varying traffic loads.
  - **Latency:** Optimize your model and serving infrastructure for low latency.

- **Security:** Implement security measures to protect your model and data.
- **Monitoring:** Monitor model performance and infrastructure health.
- **Cost:** Consider the cost of cloud resources and optimize for efficiency.

- **Personal Insight:** "Cloud deployment allows you to make your AI models accessible to a wider audience. Containerization and API endpoints simplify the process and enable seamless integration with other applications."

- **Practical Applications:**
  - **Image Recognition APIs:** Providing image recognition services to other applications.
  - **Natural Language Processing APIs:** Offering text analysis and generation capabilities.
  - **Recommendation Engines:** Deploying recommendation models for e-commerce or content platforms.
  - **Real-time Fraud Detection:** Deploying fraud detection models for financial applications.

10.2: Building Scalable AI Applications

We're now focusing on building AI applications that can handle increasing workloads and user demands. This section will guide you through the principles and practices of creating scalable AI systems.

Scalability: Handling Growth and Demand

Building AI applications that can scale is crucial for real-world deployments.Let's explore the key concepts and techniques.

- **Key Concepts:**
  - **Horizontal Scaling:** Adding more machines or instances to distribute the workload.
  - **Vertical Scaling:** Increasing the resources (CPU, memory) of a single machine.
  - **Load Balancing:** Distributing incoming traffic across multiple servers.
  - **Asynchronous Processing:** Handling tasks in the background to avoid blocking the main application.
  - **Caching:** Storing frequently accessed data to reduce database load.
  - **Microservices Architecture:** Breaking down applications into smaller, independent services.
  - **Auto-Scaling:** Automatically adjusting resources based on demand.
- **Building Scalable AI Systems:**
  - **Containerization (Docker):** Package the AI application and its dependencies into containers for consistent deployment.
  - **Orchestration (Kubernetes):** Use Kubernetes to manage and scale containerized applications.
  - **Load Balancing:** Implement load balancing to distribute traffic across multiple instances.
  - **Asynchronous Processing (Celery, RabbitMQ):** Use message queues and task queues to handle background tasks.
  - **Caching (Redis, Memcached):** Implement caching to reduce database load and improve response times.
  - **Microservices:** Break down the AI application into smaller, independent services.

- ○ **Auto-Scaling:** Configure auto-scaling to automatically adjust resources based on demand.
- **Practical Implementation (Conceptual Example with Flask and Celery):**
  - ○ We'll demonstrate a basic example using Flask and Celery for asynchronous processing.
  - ○ **Flask App (app.py):**
- Python
  - ○ from flask import Flask, request, jsonify
  - ○ from celery import Celery
  - ○ import time
  - ○
  - ○ app = Flask(__name__)
  - ○ celery = Celery(app.name, broker='redis://localhost:6379/0', backend='redis://localhost:6379/0')
  - ○
  - ○ @celery.task
  - ○ def process_data(data):
  - ○   # Simulate a long-running AI task
  - ○   time.sleep(5)
  - ○   return f"Processed: {data}"
  - ○
  - ○ @app.route('/process', methods=['POST'])
  - ○ def process():
  - ○   data = request.get_json()
  - ○   task = process_data.delay(data)
  - ○   return jsonify({'task_id': task.id}), 202
  - ○

```python
@app.route('/status/<task_id>', methods=['GET'])
def status(task_id):
    task = process_data.AsyncResult(task_id)
    if task.ready():
        return jsonify({'result': task.result})
    else:
        return jsonify({'status': 'pending'})

if __name__ == '__main__':
    app.run(debug=True, host='0.0.0.0', port=5000)
```

- **Celery Worker (worker.py):**

- Python

```python
from celery import Celery

app = Celery('tasks', broker='redis://localhost:6379/0',
backend='redis://localhost:6379/0')
```

- **Running the Application:**

- Bash

```bash
# Run Redis
redis-server

# Run Celery worker
celery -A worker.app worker --loglevel=info

# Run Flask app
```

- python app.py
-
    - **Explanation:** This example demonstrates how to use Celery to offload long-running AI tasks to a background worker. The Flask app handles incoming requests and sends tasks to Celery, which processes them asynchronously.
- **Cloud Platform Considerations:**
    - **Auto-Scaling Groups (AWS), Managed Instance Groups (Google Cloud):** Use these services to automatically scale your application instances based on demand.
    - **Load Balancers (AWS ELB, Google Cloud Load Balancing):** Use load balancers to distribute traffic across multiple instances.
    - **Managed Kubernetes Services (AWS EKS, Google Kubernetes Engine):** Use managed Kubernetes services to simplify the deployment and scaling of containerized applications.
    - **Serverless Functions (AWS Lambda, Google Cloud Functions):** Use serverless functions for event-driven AI tasks.
    - **Cloud Caching Services (AWS ElastiCache, Google Cloud Memorystore):** Use cloud caching services to improve performance.
- **Key Considerations:**
    - **Performance Monitoring:** Implement monitoring to track application performance and identify bottlenecks.
    - **Fault Tolerance:** Design your application to handle failures and ensure high availability.
    - **Cost Optimization:** Optimize resource usage to minimize cloud costs.

- Security: Implement security measures to protect your application and data.
  - Data Consistency: Ensure data consistency across multiple instances.
- Personal Insight: "Building scalable AI applications requires careful planning and design. Containerization, orchestration, and asynchronous processing are essential tools for handling increasing workloads and user demands."
- Practical Applications:
  - Real-time Recommendation Systems: Handling high volumes of user requests.
  - Large-scale Image Processing: Processing millions of images efficiently.
  - Natural Language Processing APIs: Serving NLP models to a large number of users.
  - Fraud Detection Systems: Processing real-time transactions.

10.3: Containerization with Docker for AI Deployment

Hey there, AI containerizers! We're now focusing on Docker, a powerful tool for packaging and deploying AI applications. This section will guide you through the concepts and practical implementations of using Docker for AI model deployment.

Docker: Your AI Deployment Packaging Tool

Docker simplifies the deployment process by packaging AI models and their dependencies into portable containers. Let's explore how to leverage Docker for efficient and consistent deployments.

- Key Concepts:

- **Containers:** Lightweight, standalone, executable packages of software that include everything needed to run an application: code, runtime, system tools, system libraries and settings.
- **Images:** Read-only templates with instructions for creating a Docker container.
- **Dockerfiles:** Text files with instructions for building Docker images.
- **Docker Hub:** A registry for sharing and storing Docker images.
- **Docker Compose:** A tool for defining and running multi-container Docker applications.

- **Dockerizing AI Models:**
  - **Create a Dockerfile:** Define the environment and dependencies for your AI model.
  - **Build the Docker Image:** Use the Dockerfile to create a Docker image.
  - **Run the Docker Container:** Start a container from the Docker image.
  - **Expose an API:** Implement an API endpoint to access your model within the container.

- **Practical Implementation (Docker and Flask for a Simple AI Model):**
  - We'll demonstrate a basic example using Docker and Flask to serve a simple scikit-learn model.
  - **Model Saving (Conceptual):**
- Python

```
# Sample model (conceptual)

import pickle
```

```python
from sklearn.linear_model import LinearRegression

model = LinearRegression()

# Train the model...

pickle.dump(model, open('model.pkl', 'wb'))
```

-
  - **Flask API (app.py):**
- Python

```python
from flask import Flask, request, jsonify

import pickle

import numpy as np

app = Flask(__name__)

model = pickle.load(open('model.pkl', 'rb'))

@app.route('/predict', methods=['POST'])

def predict():

    data = request.get_json()
```

```python
    input_data = np.array(data['input']).reshape(1, -1)

    prediction = model.predict(input_data).tolist()

    return jsonify({'prediction': prediction})


if __name__ == '__main__':

    app.run(debug=True, host='0.0.0.0', port=5000)
```

-
    - **Dockerfile:**
- Dockerfile

```dockerfile
FROM python:3.8-slim


WORKDIR /app


COPY requirements.txt .

RUN pip install -r requirements.txt


COPY . .
```

EXPOSE 5000

CMD ["python", "app.py"]

-
  - **requirements.txt:**
- Plaintext

Flask

scikit-learn

numpy

-
  - **Building and Running the Docker Container:**
- Bash

```bash
# Build the Docker image

docker build -t my-model-api .


# Run the Docker container

docker run -p 5000:5000 my-model-api
```

-

- **Explanation:** This example packages a Flask API for a scikit-learn model into a Docker container. The Dockerfile sets up a Python environment, installs dependencies, copies the application code, and runs the Flask app.

- **Benefits of Docker for AI Deployment:**
  - **Consistency:** Ensures consistent deployments across different environments.
  - **Portability:** Allows AI models to be easily deployed on any platform that supports Docker.
  - **Isolation:** Isolates AI models from the host system, preventing conflicts.
  - **Scalability:** Simplifies the scaling of AI applications.
  - **Reproducibility:** Makes it easy to reproduce deployments.

- **Key Considerations:**
  - **Image Size:** Optimize Docker images to minimize their size.
  - **Security:** Implement security best practices for Docker containers.
  - **Dependencies:** Manage dependencies carefully to avoid conflicts.
  - **Networking:** Configure networking to allow communication between containers.
  - **Storage:** Manage storage for persistent data.

- **Personal Insight:** "Docker simplifies AI model deployment by providing a consistent and portable environment. By packaging your model and its dependencies into a container, you can ensure that it runs reliably on any platform."

- **Practical Applications:**
  - Deploying AI models as microservices.
  - Creating reproducible environments for AI development and testing.
  - Packaging AI models for cloud deployment.
  - Building CI/CD pipelines for AI applications.

Chapter 11: Ethical AI and Responsible Development

We've learned how to build powerful AI models, but with great power comes great responsibility. This chapter is all about ensuring our AI creations are fair, safe, and beneficial to society. We'll explore addressing bias, ensuring data privacy, and developing AI ethically. Let's build AI we can be proud of!

11.1: Addressing Bias and Fairness in AI Models

We're now tackling a crucial aspect of AI development: addressing bias and ensuring fairness. This section will guide you through the concepts, challenges, and practical approaches to building equitable AI systems.

Bias and Fairness: Building Responsible AI

Bias in AI models can lead to unfair or discriminatory outcomes, which is a serious ethical concern.Let's explore how to mitigate bias and promote fairness.

- **Understanding Bias in AI:**
  - **Data Bias:** Bias present in the training data, reflecting existing societal biases.
  - **Algorithmic Bias:** Bias introduced by the design or implementation of the AI algorithm.
  - **Interaction Bias:** Bias arising from how users interact with the AI system.
  - **Evaluation Bias:** Bias in the way models are evaluated.

- **Fairness Metrics:**
  - **Demographic Parity:** Ensuring equal outcomes across different demographic groups.
  - **Equalized Odds:** Ensuring equal true positive and false positive rates across groups.
  - **Equal Opportunity:** Ensuring equal true positive rates across groups.
  - **Calibration:** Ensuring that the model's predicted probabilities match the actual probabilities.
- **Mitigating Bias:**
  - **Data Preprocessing:**
    - **Data Auditing:** Analyze the training data for potential biases.
    - **Data Augmentation:** Balance the dataset by adding underrepresented data.
    - **Reweighing:** Assign different weights to data points to balance their influence.
  - **Algorithmic Adjustments:**
    - **In-processing:** Modify the model's training process to incorporate fairness constraints.
    - **Post-processing:** Adjust the model's outputs to achieve fairness after training.
    - **Adversarial Debiasing:** Train a model to be invariant to sensitive attributes.
  - **Evaluation and Monitoring:**
    - **Fairness Audits:** Regularly evaluate the model's fairness using appropriate metrics.
    - **Continuous Monitoring:** Monitor the model's performance and fairness in real-world deployments.

- **Practical Implementation (Conceptual Example with Scikit-learn and AIF360):**
  - We'll demonstrate a basic example using Scikit-learn and AIF360 to detect and mitigate bias.
  - **Load and Preprocess Data (Conceptual):**
- Python

```python
import pandas as pd

from sklearn.model_selection import train_test_split


# Load your dataset

df = pd.read_csv('your_data.csv')


# Preprocess your data (handle missing values, encode categorical variables, etc.)

# ...


# Split data into training and testing sets

X_train, X_test, y_train, y_test = train_test_split(df.drop('target', axis=1),
df['target'], test_size=0.2, random_state=42)
```

-
  - **Train a Model (Conceptual):**

- Python

```python
from sklearn.linear_model import LogisticRegression


# Train a logistic regression model

model = LogisticRegression()

model.fit(X_train, y_train)
```

-
  - **Evaluate Fairness with AIF360 (Conceptual):**
- Python

```python
from aif360.datasets import BinaryLabelDataset

from aif360.metrics import BinaryLabelDatasetMetric


# Create BinaryLabelDataset

dataset_train = BinaryLabelDataset(df=pd.concat([X_train, y_train], axis=1), label_names=['target'], protected_attribute_names=['sensitive_attribute'])


# Calculate fairness metrics
```

```python
metric_train = BinaryLabelDatasetMetric(dataset_train,
unprivileged_groups=[{'sensitive_attribute': 0}],
privileged_groups=[{'sensitive_attribute': 1}])


print("Statistical Parity Difference:", metric_train.statistical_parity_difference())
```

-

    - **Mitigate Bias with AIF360 (Conceptual):**
- Python

```python
from aif360.algorithms.preprocessing import Reweighing


# Apply reweighing to mitigate bias

reweighing = Reweighing(unprivileged_groups=[{'sensitive_attribute': 0}],
privileged_groups=[{'sensitive_attribute': 1}])

dataset_train_transformed = reweighing.fit_transform(dataset_train)


# Train a new model with reweighed data

# ...
```

   - **Explanation:** This example demonstrates how to use AIF360 to calculate fairness metrics and apply reweighing to mitigate bias.

Remember to replace placeholder code with your actual data and model.

- **Key Considerations:**
  - **Contextual Fairness:** Fairness is context-dependent and requires careful consideration of the specific application.
  - **Trade-offs:** Fairness interventions may involve trade-offs with other performance metrics.
  - **Transparency and Explainability:** AI models should be transparent and explainable to facilitate fairness audits.
  - **Stakeholder Involvement:** Involve stakeholders from diverse backgrounds in the development and evaluation of AI systems.
  - **Legal and Regulatory Compliance:** Be aware of legal and regulatory requirements related to fairness and bias.

- **Personal Insight:** "Building fair AI models is an ongoing challenge that requires a multidisciplinary approach. It's crucial to consider fairness throughout the AI development lifecycle, from data collection to deployment."

- **Practical Applications:**
  - **Credit Scoring:** Ensuring fair access to credit for all demographic groups.
  - **Hiring Systems:** Mitigating bias in resume screening and candidate selection.
  - **Criminal Justice:** Addressing bias in risk assessment tools.
  - **Healthcare:** Ensuring equitable access to healthcare resources.

11.2: Ensuring Data Privacy and Security

We're now focusing on a critical aspect of AI development: ensuring data privacy and security. This section will guide you through the concepts, challenges, and practical approaches to protecting sensitive information in AI systems.

Data Privacy and Security: Building Trust in AI

Protecting user data is paramount for building trust in AI systems. Let's explore how to implement robust privacy and security measures.

- **Understanding Data Privacy and Security:**
  - **Data Privacy:** Protecting sensitive information from unauthorized access or disclosure.
  - **Data Security:** Protecting data from unauthorized access, use, disclosure, disruption, modification, or destruction.
  - **Key Principles:**
    - **Data Minimization:** Collecting only the data necessary for the task.
    - **Purpose Limitation:** Using data only for the intended purpose.
    - **Data Anonymization/Pseudonymization:** Removing or obscuring personally identifiable information.
    - **Data Encryption:** Encrypting data at rest and in transit.
    - **Access Control:** Restricting access to sensitive data based on roles and permissions.
- **Privacy-Enhancing Techniques:**
  - **Differential Privacy:** Adding noise to data to protect individual privacy while preserving statistical properties.

- Federated Learning: Training models on decentralized data without sharing raw data.
- Homomorphic Encryption: Performing computations on encrypted data without decrypting it.
- Secure Multi-Party Computation (SMPC): Enabling multiple parties to compute a function on their private inputs without revealing them.

- **Security Best Practices:**
  - **Data Encryption:** Encrypting sensitive data at rest and in transit.
  - **Access Control:** Implementing strong access controls and authentication mechanisms.
  - **Regular Security Audits:** Conducting regular security assessments to identify vulnerabilities.
  - **Incident Response Planning:** Developing a plan for responding to security incidents.
  - **Software Updates:** Keeping software and libraries up-to-date with security patches.

- **Practical Implementation (Conceptual Example with Differential Privacy):**
  - We'll demonstrate a basic example of differential privacy using the diffprivlib library.
  - **Install** diffprivlib:
- Bash
  - pip install diffprivlib
-

  - **Apply Differential Privacy:**
- Python

```python
import numpy as np
from diffprivlib.mechanisms import Gaussian
from diffprivlib.utils import PrivacyBudget

# Sample data
data = np.array([1, 2, 3, 4, 5, 6, 7, 8, 9, 10])

# Differential privacy parameters
epsilon = 1.0  # Privacy budget
delta = 1e-5  # Probability of failure

# Create a Gaussian mechanism
mech = Gaussian(epsilon=epsilon, delta=delta)

# Apply differential privacy to the mean
noisy_mean = mech.randomise(np.mean(data))

print("Original Mean:", np.mean(data))
print("Noisy Mean (Differential Privacy):", noisy_mean)
```

- **Explanation:** This example demonstrates how to add noise to the mean of a dataset using differential privacy. The Gaussian mechanism from diffprivlib protects individual privacy while preserving the statistical properties of the data.

- **Key Considerations:**
  - **Regulatory Compliance:** Be aware of data privacy regulations like GDPR and CCPA.

- **Data Governance:** Implement data governance policies to ensure responsible data handling.
- **Transparency and Explainability:** Be transparent about how data is used and processed.
- **User Consent:** Obtain explicit user consent for data collection and processing.
- **Ethical Considerations:** Consider the ethical implications of data collection and use.

- **Personal Insight:** "Data privacy and security are fundamental to building trust in AI systems. By implementing robust privacy-enhancing techniques and security best practices, we can protect sensitive information and foster responsible AI development."

- **Practical Applications:**
  - **Healthcare Data Analysis:** Protecting patient privacy while enabling medical research.
  - **Financial Data Analysis:** Securing sensitive financial information.
  - **Personalized Advertising:** Protecting user privacy while delivering targeted ads.
  - **Smart City Applications:** Ensuring data privacy in urban environments.

11.3: Developing AI Responsibly and Ethically

We're now focusing on the overarching principles of responsible AI development. This section will guide you through the ethical considerations, frameworks, and practical approaches to building AI systems that align with human values.

Responsible AI: Building Trustworthy and Beneficial Systems

Developing AI responsibly goes beyond technical implementation; it involves considering the societal impact and ethical implications. Let's explore the key aspects of building ethical AI.

- **Understanding Responsible AI:**
  - **Ethical Principles:**
    - **Fairness:** Ensuring equitable treatment and outcomes for all individuals.
    - **Transparency:** Making AI systems understandable and explainable.
    - **Accountability:** Establishing clear lines of responsibility for AI decisions.
    - **Privacy:** Protecting sensitive information and respecting user privacy.
    - **Safety:** Minimizing the potential for harm and unintended consequences.
    - **Human-Centeredness:** Designing AI systems that prioritize human well-being.
  - **Key Considerations:**
    - **Bias Mitigation:** Identifying and mitigating biases in data and algorithms.
    - **Explainability and Interpretability:** Making AI models understandable to humans.

- **Data Governance:** Implementing policies for responsible data collection and use.
- **Stakeholder Engagement:** Involving diverse stakeholders in the development process.
- **Impact Assessment:** Evaluating the potential social and environmental impact of AI systems.

- **Ethical Frameworks and Guidelines:**
  - **AI Ethics Principles (e.g., OECD, EU AI Ethics Guidelines):** Providing high-level guidance for responsible AI development.
  - **Industry Standards (e.g., IEEE, ISO):** Developing technical standards for ethical AI practices.
  - **Internal Policies:** Organizations developing their own ethical guidelines and procedures.

- **Practical Approaches:**
  - **Ethical Impact Assessments:**
    - Conduct assessments to identify potential ethical risks and develop mitigation strategies.
    - Involve diverse stakeholders in the assessment process.
  - **Explainable AI (XAI):**
    - Use techniques to make AI models more transparent and understandable.
    - Provide explanations for AI decisions and predictions.
  - **Bias Auditing and Mitigation:**
    - Regularly audit AI models for bias using appropriate metrics.
    - Implement techniques to mitigate bias in data and algorithms.
  - **Data Governance and Privacy:**
    - Establish clear policies for data collection, storage, and use.

- ■ Implement privacy-enhancing techniques like differential privacy and federated learning.
  - ○ **Human-in-the-Loop Systems:**
    - ■ Design AI systems that allow for human oversight and intervention.
    - ■ Provide mechanisms for users to challenge or correct AI decisions.
  - ○ **Stakeholder Engagement:**
    - ■ Involve diverse stakeholders in the development and evaluation of AI systems.
    - ■ Ensure that AI systems reflect the values and needs of the communities they serve.
- **Practical Implementation (Conceptual Example with Explainability):**
  - ○ We'll demonstrate a basic example using LIME (Local Interpretable Model-agnostic Explanations) for explainability.
  - ○ **Install LIME:**
- Bash

```
pip install lime
```

-
  - ○ **Apply LIME to a Text Classifier (Conceptual):**
- Python

```
import lime

import lime.lime_text
```

```python
from sklearn.feature_extraction.text import TfidfVectorizer

from sklearn.naive_bayes import MultinomialNB

from sklearn.pipeline import make_pipeline


# Sample dataset (replace with your actual data)

texts = ["This movie was great!", "Terrible product, I'm disappointed."]

labels = ["positive", "negative"]


# Create a pipeline

pipeline = make_pipeline(TfidfVectorizer(), MultinomialNB())

pipeline.fit(texts, labels)


# LIME explainer

explainer = lime.lime_text.LimeTextExplainer(class_names=["negative",
"positive"])


# Explain a prediction

explanation = explainer.explain_instance(texts[0], pipeline.predict_proba,
num_features=6)
```

```
# Print the explanation

print(explanation.as_list())
```

-
  - **Explanation:** This example demonstrates how to use LIME to explain a text classification prediction. LIME highlights the words that contributed most to the prediction.
- **Key Considerations:**
  - **Contextual Ethics:** Ethical considerations are context-dependent and require careful analysis.
  - **Interdisciplinary Collaboration:** Ethical AI development requires collaboration between experts from different fields.
  - **Continuous Learning:** Ethical guidelines and best practices are constantly evolving.
  - **Accountability and Responsibility:** Establish clear lines of responsibility for AI decisions.
  - **Public Engagement:** Engage with the public to build trust and understanding.
- **Personal Insight:** "Developing AI responsibly is a continuous journey that requires ongoing dialogue and collaboration. By embedding ethical considerations into every stage of AI development, we can build AI systems that benefit humanity and align with our values."
- **Practical Applications:**
  - **Healthcare AI:** Ensuring equitable access and patient safety.

- **Criminal Justice AI:** Addressing bias and ensuring fairness in legal systems.

- **Autonomous Vehicles:** Prioritizing human safety and ethical decision-making.

- **Social Media AI:** Mitigating harmful content and promoting responsible discourse.

Chapter 12: AI-Assisted Development Tools

We've covered a lot of AI concepts and techniques, but let's talk about how AI can actually help us write code. In this chapter, we'll explore AI-assisted development tools that can make our coding lives easier and more efficient. We'll cover code completion, debugging, and how to integrate these tools into our workflow. Let's make AI our coding buddy!

12.1: Leveraging AI for Code Completion and Debugging

We're now exploring how AI is revolutionizing the coding process, specifically focusing on code completion and debugging. This section will guide you through the concepts, tools, and practical implementations that are making development faster and more efficient.

AI: Your Coding Sidekick

AI is no longer just a futuristic concept; it's a practical tool that's becoming an integral part of the developer's toolkit. Let's explore how AI is enhancing code completion and debugging.

- **Understanding AI-Powered Code Completion:**
  - **Contextual Suggestions:** AI tools analyze your code in real-time to provide contextually relevant suggestions.
  - **Pattern Recognition:** AI models learn from vast code repositories to recognize patterns and predict your next lines of code.
  - **Reduced Boilerplate:** AI can generate repetitive code, freeing you to focus on more complex tasks.

- ○ **Improved Accuracy:** AI can often provide more accurate and relevant suggestions than traditional code completion tools.
- **Understanding AI-Assisted Debugging:**
  - ○ **Anomaly Detection:** AI can identify anomalies and potential bugs in your code.
  - ○ **Root Cause Analysis:** AI can analyze code execution and identify the root cause of errors.
  - ○ **Automated Bug Fixes:** In some cases, AI can even suggest or automatically apply bug fixes.
  - ○ **Improved Efficiency:** AI can significantly reduce the time and effort required for debugging.
- **Key Tools and Technologies:**
  - ○ **GitHub Copilot:** AI pair programmer that offers code suggestions and completions within your IDE.
  - ○ **Tabnine:** AI code completion tool that learns from your coding patterns.
  - ○ **DeepCode (now Snyk Code):** AI-powered code analysis tool that identifies potential bugs and security vulnerabilities.
  - ○ **MutableAI:** Tool that helps with code generation and modification via natural language.
  - ○ **Amazon CodeWhisperer:** AI coding companion that generates real-time single-line and full-function code suggestions.
- **Practical Implementation (Conceptual Example with GitHub Copilot-like Behavior):**
  - ○ While GitHub Copilot is an IDE extension, we can conceptually illustrate its functionality with a simple example:
- Python

```python
# Conceptual Example (GitHub Copilot-like behavior)

def find_max(numbers):
    """
    Finds the maximum number in a list.
    """
    # Copilot might suggest:
    if not numbers:
        return None
    max_num = numbers[0]
    for num in numbers:
        if num > max_num:
            max_num = num
    return max_num


# Example Usage
numbers = [10, 5, 20, 15]
maximum = find_max(numbers)
print(f"Maximum: {maximum}")
```

-
  - **Explanation:** In a real IDE with Copilot, as you type the function signature and docstring, Copilot would suggest the code for finding the maximum number.
- **Practical Implementation (Conceptual Example with AI-Assisted Debugging):**
  - While AI-assisted debugging is often integrated into IDEs or specialized tools, we can conceptualize how it might work:
- Python

```python
# Conceptual Example (AI-assisted debugging)

def divide(a, b):

    # Potential bug: division by zero

    return a / b



def debug_divide(a, b):

    # AI-assisted debugging might suggest:

    if b == 0:

        print("Error: Division by zero")

        return None # Or raise an exception.

    else:
```

```
    return a / b


# Example Usage

result = debug_divide(10, 0)

if result is not None:

    print(f"Result: {result}")
```

-
  - **Explanation:** An AI-powered debugger could analyze the `divide` function and suggest adding a check for division by zero.
- **Key Considerations:**
  - **Code Quality:** AI suggestions should be reviewed to ensure they meet code quality standards.
  - **Security:** Be cautious of AI-generated code that might introduce security vulnerabilities.
  - **Privacy:** Be mindful of data privacy when using AI tools that collect code data.
  - **Contextual Understanding:** AI tools should be able to understand the context of your code.
  - **Customization:** AI tools should allow for customization to fit your coding style and preferences.
- **Personal Insight:** "AI-powered code completion and debugging tools are transforming the development process by making it faster, more efficient, and less error-prone. However, it's essential to use these tools responsibly and maintain a balance between automation and human expertise."

- **Practical Applications:**
  - **Rapid Prototyping:** Quickly generate code for initial prototypes.
  - **Code Refactoring:** Automate repetitive refactoring tasks.
  - **Bug Prevention:** Identify potential bugs before they cause problems.
  - **Learning New Languages:** AI can help you learn new programming languages by providing relevant code examples.

You've now learned how AI is enhancing code completion and debugging. Remember to use these tools responsibly, review AI-generated code, and be aware of the potential risks and benefits.

12.2: Integrating AI Tools into the Development Workflow

We're now diving into the practical aspects of integrating AI tools into the development workflow. This section will guide you through the strategies, best practices, and considerations for seamless integration.

AI in Your Workflow: Streamlining Development

Integrating AI tools into the development workflow can significantly enhance productivity and efficiency. Let's explore how to make this integration successful.

- **Understanding Workflow Integration:**
  - **Seamless Integration:** Ensuring AI tools work smoothly within existing development environments and processes.
  - **Automation:** Automating repetitive tasks to free up developer time for more complex tasks.
  - **Contextual Assistance:** Providing AI assistance that is relevant to the current task and context.

- **Feedback Loops:** Incorporating feedback from developers to improve AI tool performance.
- **Continuous Integration/Continuous Delivery (CI/CD):** Integrating AI tools into CI/CD pipelines for automated code review and testing.

- **Integration Strategies:**
    - **IDE Integration:**
        - Integrate AI tools directly into Integrated Development Environments (IDEs) for seamless code completion, analysis, and debugging.
        - Examples: IDE extensions for GitHub Copilot, Tabnine, etc.
    - **CI/CD Pipeline Integration:**
        - Integrate AI tools into CI/CD pipelines for automated code review, testing, and deployment.
        - Examples: Codiga integration with Jenkins, GitLab CI, etc.
    - **Command-Line Tools:**
        - Use command-line AI tools for specific tasks like code analysis or documentation generation.
        - Examples: Tools for static analysis integrated into build scripts.
    - **API Integration:**
        - Integrate AI tools through APIs for custom workflows and applications.
        - Examples: Using APIs for natural language to code generation.
    - **Collaboration Platforms:**
        - Integrate AI tools into collaboration platforms like Slack or Jira for automated notifications and task management.
        - Examples: AI-powered chatbots for code review or issue tracking.

- **Practical Implementation (Conceptual Example with CI/CD Integration):**
  - We'll illustrate a conceptual example of integrating AI-powered code analysis into a CI/CD pipeline using GitLab CI.
  - **GitLab CI Configuration (.gitlab-ci.yml):**
- YAML
  - stages:
  -   - test
  -   - analyze
  -
  - test:
  -   stage: test
  -   script:
  -    - pytest tests/
  -
  - analyze:
  -   stage: analyze
  -   script:
  -    - ai-code-analyzer --report code_analysis_report.json # Conceptual AI analyzer
  -   artifacts:
  -    paths:
  -     - code_analysis_report.json
  -   after_script:
  -    - echo "AI code analysis completed."
  - **Conceptual AI Code Analyzer (ai-code-analyzer):**

- Imagine ai-code-analyzer is a command-line tool that uses AI to analyze code and generate a report.
- It would identify potential bugs, security vulnerabilities, and code quality issues.
- The report (code_analysis_report.json) would be used for review and automated checks.
  - **Explanation:** This example shows how to integrate an AI code analyzer into a GitLab CI pipeline. The analyzer runs after the tests and generates a report that can be used to identify code issues.

- **Key Considerations:**
  - **Tool Compatibility:** Ensure AI tools are compatible with your existing development environment and tools.
  - **Integration Complexity:** Consider the complexity and effort required for integration.
  - **Performance Impact:** Evaluate the impact of AI tools on performance and resource usage.
  - **Data Security and Privacy:** Ensure that AI tools handle data securely and comply with privacy regulations.
  - **User Experience:** Design the integration to provide a seamless and intuitive user experience.

- **Personal Insight:** "Integrating AI tools into the development workflow requires careful planning and execution. By focusing on seamless integration, automation, and contextual assistance, you can significantly enhance developer productivity and code quality."

- **Practical Applications:**
  - **Automated Code Reviews:** Integrating AI tools to automate code reviews and identify potential issues.

- **Intelligent Issue Tracking:** Using AI to analyze issue reports and suggest solutions.
- **Automated Deployment:** Integrating AI tools into CI/CD pipelines for automated deployment.
- **Predictive Maintenance:** Using AI to predict and prevent system failures.
- **Knowledge Management:** Using AI to organize and retrieve code-related information.

You've now learned how to integrate AI tools into the development workflow. Remember to focus on seamless integration, automation, and contextual assistance to maximize the benefits of AI.

12.3: Staying Updated with Emerging AI Technologies

We're now addressing the crucial aspect of staying updated in the rapidly evolving field of AI. This section will guide you through the strategies, resources, and mindsets needed to keep pace with emerging technologies.

The AI Frontier: Continuous Learning and Adaptation

The AI landscape is dynamic, with new tools, techniques, and breakthroughs emerging constantly. Let's explore how to stay ahead of the curve.

- **Understanding the Pace of AI Evolution:**
  - **Rapid Innovation:** AI is characterized by rapid innovation and development.
  - **Interdisciplinary Nature:** AI draws from various fields, including computer science, mathematics, linguistics, and neuroscience.

- **Open-Source Contributions:** The AI community is highly collaborative, with many open-source projects and contributions.
- **Industry Adoption:** AI is being adopted across various industries, leading to new applications and use cases.

- **Strategies for Staying Updated:**
  - **Follow Key Researchers and Organizations:**
    - Stay informed about the latest research and developments from leading AI researchers and organizations.
    - Examples: DeepMind, OpenAI, Google AI, Facebook AI Research (FAIR).
  - **Engage with the AI Community:**
    - Participate in online forums, conferences, and meetups to connect with other AI practitioners.
    - Examples: Reddit's r/MachineLearning, NeurIPS, ICML.
  - **Explore Open-Source Projects:**
    - Learn from and contribute to open-source AI projects to gain hands-on experience.
    - Examples: TensorFlow, PyTorch, scikit-learn, Hugging Face Transformers.
  - **Take Online Courses and Tutorials:**
    - Enroll in online courses and tutorials to learn about new AI technologies and techniques.
    - Examples: Coursera, edX, Udacity, fast.ai.
  - **Read Research Papers and Publications:**
    - Stay up-to-date with the latest research by reading academic papers and publications.

- Examples: arXiv, Journal of Machine Learning Research (JMLR).
    - ○ **Experiment with New Tools and Technologies:**
        - Experiment with new AI tools and technologies to gain practical experience and insights.
        - Examples: Cloud AI platforms, pre-trained models, AI APIs.
    - ○ **Build Personal Projects:**
        - Apply your knowledge by building personal AI projects to reinforce learning and explore new ideas.
        - Examples: Building a chatbot, training an image classifier, developing a recommendation system.
- **Practical Implementation (Conceptual Example with Hugging Face Transformers):**
    - ○ We'll demonstrate a conceptual example of using Hugging Face Transformers for a new task:
    - ○ **Install Transformers:**
- Bash

```
pip install transformers
```

- ○ **Use a Pre-trained Model:**
- Python

```
from transformers import pipeline
```

```
# Conceptual example: Using a new model for a novel task

novel_task_pipeline = pipeline("text-generation",
model="some-new-model/novel-task") # Replace with actual model


# Generate text

text = novel_task_pipeline("Write a short story about AI and the future.")


print(text[0]['generated_text'])
```

- **Explanation:** This example shows how to use a pre-trained model from Hugging Face Transformers for a novel task (text generation). Replace "some-new-model/novel-task" with an actual model identifier.

- **Key Considerations:**
  - **Filter Information:** Be discerning about the information you consume, as there's a lot of hype and misinformation.
  - **Focus on Fundamentals:** Understand the fundamental concepts of AI to better grasp new developments.
  - **Prioritize Practical Skills:** Focus on developing practical skills that are in demand.
  - **Network and Collaborate:** Build relationships with other AI practitioners and collaborate on projects.
  - **Embrace Lifelong Learning:** Adopt a mindset of continuous learning and adaptation.

- **Personal Insight:** "Staying updated in the AI field requires a proactive and curious mindset. By engaging with the community, exploring open-source projects, and experimenting with new technologies, you can stay ahead of the curve and contribute to the advancement of AI."

- **Practical Applications:**
  - **Personalized Learning:** Using AI to curate personalized learning resources.
  - **Knowledge Graphs:** Building knowledge graphs to organize and retrieve AI-related information.
  - **AI-Powered News Aggregators:** Developing tools to filter and summarize AI news and research.
  - **Virtual Mentors:** Creating AI-powered virtual mentors to guide AI learners.

Your AI Learning Journey

You've now learned how to stay updated with emerging AI technologies. Remember to engage with the community, explore open-source projects, and prioritize practical skills. Let's continue to explore the future of AI.

Chapter 13: Practical AI Projects and Exercises

We've covered a lot of theory and techniques, and now it's time to roll up our sleeves and build some real-world AI projects. This chapter is all about applying your knowledge to practical problems and solidifying your understanding. We'll explore several project examples and provide comprehensive solutions and explanations. Let's build some cool AI projects!

13.1: Real-World AI Project Examples

Hey there, AI innovators! We're now diving into the realm of real-world AI projects, showcasing how AI is making a tangible impact across various industries. This section will guide you through practical examples, highlighting the challenges, solutions, and key takeaways.

AI in Action: Transforming Industries and Lives

Real-world AI projects often involve complex challenges and require a multidisciplinary approach. Let's explore a few examples.

- **Example 1: AI-Powered Medical Diagnosis System**
    - **Problem:** Early and accurate diagnosis of diseases from medical images (e.g., X-rays, MRIs).
    - **Solution:**
        - Develop a Convolutional Neural Network (CNN) to analyze medical images.
        - Train the CNN on a large dataset of labeled images.
        - Integrate the model into a clinical workflow for real-time diagnosis assistance.
    -

- ○ **Key Technologies:**
  - ■ TensorFlow/PyTorch for CNN development.
  - ■ Medical imaging libraries (e.g., SimpleITK).
  - ■ Cloud platforms for scalable deployment.
- ○ **Practical Implementation (Conceptual):**
- Python

```python
# Conceptual example (CNN for medical image analysis)

import tensorflow as tf

from tensorflow.keras.models import Sequential

from tensorflow.keras.layers import Conv2D, MaxPooling2D, Flatten, Dense


# Load and preprocess medical images...

# ...


# Define the CNN model

model = Sequential([

    Conv2D(32, (3, 3), activation='relu', input_shape=(image_height, image_width, image_channels)),

    MaxPooling2D((2, 2)),
```

```
# ... more layers

Flatten(),

Dense(128, activation='relu'),

Dense(num_classes, activation='softmax')

])


# Compile and train the model...

# ...


# Integrate with clinical workflow...

# ...
```

- ○ **Expert Commentary:** "AI-powered medical diagnosis systems have the potential to improve patient outcomes by enabling early and accurate disease detection.However, it's crucial to address ethical considerations related to data privacy and model bias."
- **Example 2: AI-Driven Personalized Recommendation Engine**
  - ○ **Problem:** Providing personalized recommendations to users on e-commerce platforms or content streaming services.
  - ○ **Solution:**
    - ■ Develop a collaborative filtering or content-based recommendation system.

- Train the model on user interaction data (e.g., purchase history, viewing history).
- Deploy the model as an API for real-time recommendations.
  - **Key Technologies:**
    - Scikit-learn/TensorFlow Recommenders for recommendation algorithms.
    - Database systems for user data storage.
    - API frameworks (e.g., Flask, FastAPI).
  - **Practical Implementation (Conceptual):**
- Python

```python
# Conceptual example (collaborative filtering)

from sklearn.metrics.pairwise import cosine_similarity


# Load user interaction data...

# ...


# Calculate user similarity matrix

user_similarity = cosine_similarity(user_data)


# Generate recommendations...
```

...

Deploy as an API...

...

-
  - **Personal Insight:** "Personalized recommendation engines enhance user experience and drive engagement. However, it's important to consider ethical implications related to filter bubbles and content diversity."
- **Example 3: AI-Enabled Smart City Traffic Management**
  - **Problem:** Optimizing traffic flow and reducing congestion in urban areas.
  - **Solution:**
    - Develop an AI model to analyze traffic data from sensors and cameras.
    - Implement real-time traffic signal control based on the model's predictions.
    - Integrate the system with existing city infrastructure.
  - **Key Technologies:**
    - Time-series forecasting models (e.g., LSTMs).
    - Computer vision for traffic analysis.
    - IoT platforms for sensor data integration.
  - **Practical Implementation (Conceptual):**
- Python

```
# Conceptual example (LSTM for traffic forecasting)

import tensorflow as tf

from tensorflow.keras.models import Sequential

from tensorflow.keras.layers import LSTM, Dense


# Load traffic data...

# ...


# Define the LSTM model

model = Sequential([

    LSTM(units=50, return_sequences=True, input_shape=(time_steps, features)),

    LSTM(units=50),

    Dense(units=1)

])


# Train and deploy the model...

# ...
```

- **Concise Explanation:** Smart city traffic management systems can improve urban mobility and reduce environmental impact. However, it's crucial to address privacy concerns related to surveillance and data collection.
- **Key Considerations for Real-World Projects:**
  - **Data Quality and Availability:** Real-world projects often require large and diverse datasets.
  - **Scalability and Performance:** AI systems must be designed to handle real-time data and high traffic loads.
  - **Robustness and Reliability:** AI systems must be robust to noise and errors in real-world environments.
  - **Ethical Considerations:** AI projects must address ethical concerns related to bias, privacy, and safety.
  - **Integration with Existing Systems:** AI systems must be integrated with existing infrastructure and workflows.

13.2: Comprehensive Project Solutions and Explanations

We're now diving into the art of crafting comprehensive project solutions, providing in-depth explanations, and addressing potential challenges. This section will guide you through the process of developing robust AI projects with clear and actionable insights.

Building End-to-End AI Solutions: From Concept to Deployment

Creating successful AI projects involves more than just building models; it requires a holistic approach that encompasses data, infrastructure, and deployment. Let's explore how to develop comprehensive solutions.

- **Project Example: AI-Powered Customer Churn Prediction System**
  - ○ **Problem:** Predict customer churn for a subscription-based service to implement retention strategies.
  - ○ **Solution:**
    1. **Data Collection and Preprocessing:**
       - ■ Gather customer data (e.g., usage patterns, demographics, support interactions).
       - ■ Clean and preprocess the data (handle missing values, encode categorical variables).
       - ■ Split the data into training, validation, and testing sets.
    2. **Feature Engineering:**
       - ■ Create relevant features (e.g., average usage per month, time since last interaction).
       - ■ Use domain knowledge to create meaningful features.
    3. **Model Selection and Training:**
       - ■ Choose a suitable model (e.g., logistic regression, random forest, gradient boosting).
       - ■ Train the model on the training data and tune hyperparameters using validation data.
    4. **Model Evaluation:**
       - ■ Evaluate the model's performance using appropriate metrics (e.g., precision, recall, F1-score, AUC).
       - ■ Analyze the model's predictions and identify areas for improvement.
    5. **Deployment and Integration:**
       - ■ Deploy the model as an API using Flask or FastAPI.
       - ■ Integrate the API with the company's CRM system.

- Implement real-time or batch prediction pipelines.

6. **Monitoring and Maintenance:**
   - Monitor the model's performance in production.
   - Retrain the model periodically with new data.
   - Address any issues or biases that arise.

- **Practical Implementation (Conceptual):**
- Python

```python
# Conceptual example: Customer churn prediction pipeline

import pandas as pd

from sklearn.model_selection import train_test_split

from sklearn.ensemble import RandomForestClassifier

from sklearn.metrics import classification_report

from flask import Flask, request, jsonify

import pickle


# 1. Data Collection and Preprocessing

df = pd.read_csv("customer_data.csv")

# ... preprocessing steps ...

X = df.drop("churn", axis=1)
```

```python
y = df["churn"]

X_train, X_test, y_train, y_test = train_test_split(X, y, test_size=0.2,
random_state=42)


# 2. Feature Engineering

# ... feature creation ...


# 3. Model Selection and Training

model = RandomForestClassifier(random_state=42)

model.fit(X_train, y_train)


# 4. Model Evaluation

y_pred = model.predict(X_test)

print(classification_report(y_test, y_pred))


# 5. Deployment (Flask API)

app = Flask(__name__)

pickle.dump(model, open("churn_model.pkl", "wb"))
```

```python
loaded_model = pickle.load(open("churn_model.pkl", "rb"))


@app.route("/predict", methods=["POST"])

def predict():

    data = request.get_json()

    prediction = loaded_model.predict([data["features"]])

    return jsonify({"churn_prediction": int(prediction[0])})


if __name__ == "__main__":

    app.run(debug=True)


# 6. Monitoring and Maintenance

# ... monitoring and retraining ...
```

-
  - ○ **Expert Commentary:** "Developing a comprehensive churn prediction system requires a holistic approach that covers data handling, model development, deployment, and maintenance.Continuous monitoring and retraining are crucial for long-term success."
- **Key Considerations for Comprehensive Solutions:**

- **Data Quality and Availability:** Ensure high-quality and relevant data.
- **Model Explainability:** Make the model's predictions understandable to stakeholders.
- **Scalability and Performance:** Design the system to handle increasing data and user loads.
- **Security and Privacy:** Implement security measures to protect sensitive data.
- **Integration with Existing Systems:** Ensure seamless integration with existing infrastructure.
- **User Experience:** Design the system with a focus on user experience.
- **Ethical Implications:** Address potential ethical concerns related to bias and fairness.

- **Personal Insight:** "Building comprehensive AI solutions is a collaborative effort that requires expertise from various domains. By focusing on data quality, model explainability, and ethical considerations, you can create AI systems that provide real value and build trust."

- **Practical Applications:**
  - **Supply Chain Optimization:** Developing AI systems to optimize inventory management and logistics.
  - **Financial Fraud Detection:** Building AI models to detect and prevent fraudulent transactions.
  - **Personalized Learning Platforms:** Creating AI-powered platforms that adapt to individual learning styles.
  - **Environmental Monitoring Systems:** Developing AI systems to analyze environmental data and predict pollution levels.

Your AI Solution Architect Guide

You've now learned how to develop comprehensive AI project solutions. Remember to focus on data quality, model explainability, and ethical considerations to build robust and trustworthy AI systems.